London 04/02/2025

Welcome in

MULTIDIMENSIONAL WINE

An initiation

GÉRARD BERTRAND

MULTIDIMENSIONAL WINE

An initiation

EDITIONS
ORIGINE
nature

To all those who have helped, are helping, and will help
the soul of our terroirs and our wines to shine.

Foreword

The time has come to share with humility, fervour, and passion four decades of my experience with vintages, foundational encounters, conquests, and obstacles overcome. My life journey continues the adventure quietly started by my grandmother, Paule Bertrand, in 1920, and consolidated by my father, Georges Bertrand, from 1962 to 1987.

This family heritage, with its values of constant improvement and courage, has guided my steps and given me the necessary strength to face multiple challenges. I quickly understood the need to forge the way for a Languedoc viticulture committed to excellence.

This testimony aims to present, in an original and quirky way, a unique and collective approach guided by an existential quest. The strength of the intention prompted the exploration of a new way, blending artistic endeavour, biodynamic viticulture, and a deep-seated feeling for the truth. The vision came into focus, strategy paved the way, action plans enabled international development, and human and financial resources boosted implementation, all to reach ambitious goals.

Then the world changed. The complexity of markets, geopolitical issues, the arrival of new technologies, competition with spirit and beer brands all now necessitate the use of disruptive business models containing powerful and authentic messages.

The spirit descends into matter and sometimes creates the right conditions for impetus at the service of a fertile imagination.

A multidimensional wine is a drink that feeds the heart of humankind and fosters transcendence, new energy, and an unprecedented vibrational movement. The art of blending has revealed in me the desire to share the secrets and hidden treasures of our terroirs while pushing back the limits imposed by conventional winemaking. This pathway informs an expertise that results from the exploration of the different universes which have been part of my personal and professional journeys. Sport, viticulture, art, hospitality, events, but also wine-related, economic, ecological, political, or philosophical encounters have informed my own journey.

A multidimensional wine is a drink that feeds the heart of humankind and fosters transcendence, new energy, and an unprecedented vibrational movement.

I am a citizen of the world, a French and Occitan patriot, but the heart of my childhood self remains forever tied to the Corbières region. Its arid earth dotted with Cathar castles, and rolling and fragrant hills, are part of my DNA and magnify my sensitivity, as well as my will to create and act in harmony with the chivalrous spirit of our ancestors.

A multidimensional wine is also the continuation of the history and the origins of a viticultural estate or parcel, unveiled in full conscience by painstaking work and an iconoclastic and spiritual approach.

CHAPTER 1

FUNDAMENTALS

In vino veritas

Blending is the Everest of the winemaker, the *Opera Vertical* which calls into question previous achievements, and demands thorough preparation to conquer new faces of the same mountain, every single year. There is nothing more beautiful or more exhilarating in wine. It is the pinnacle, the ultimate act, and it is what reveals the imprint of the vintage.

There are different schools of thought when it comes to blending. There are those who keep to the same trusted recipes passed down over generations with the conviction that nature has already revealed its full potential. Those not blessed with a refined palate prefer to delegate blending to the house winemaker. And finally, there are the experts who want to be the ones to unlock the new vintage themselves. In any case, seeking the advice of a consultant or the winery's technical teams is recommended, as achieving the perfect blend is always a collective effort. The subtle, yet essential, skill of the master of ceremonies is the willingness to embody the role of orchestra conductor. I like to ensure that everybody is playing from the same score with different yet complementary sensibilities.

In the world of art, for example, of sculpture, the blend of different materials and shapes conveys a multidimensional and timeless approach. In the world of wine, using the same grape variety grown on different plots, or using different grape varieties, opens the door to different creative rationales. Using the same grape variety requires an asceticism and a rather academic relationship with the history of the land of its provenance, whereas using different grape varieties leads to a constant renewal of proportions and balances, in parallel with the search for continuity and a unique message. The winemaker, imbued with artistic fervour, and figuring out their wine virtually out of nowhere, will be guided by a constant flux of subconscious suggestions and will in turn be able to guide his team on the path to deliverance.

Since my earliest childhood, I have been inspired by Dionysus. My father Georges, and my mum Geneviève, roamed the Corbières, the Minervois, and the Roussillon to collect samples from winegrowers and cooperatives. In the seventies, the history of a revived Languedoc was being written by powerful and heady red wines, influenced by their terroirs. Georges Bertrand methodically tasted two hundred wine samples per day and my mum would score them between 1 and 10. Every now and again, he would pause to contemplate a wine different from the others, more balanced and more elegant. A few flowery tasting notes would then be added to the scores. I was a watchful child, inquisitive and fascinated by those wines' capacity to enchant my father and stop him in his tracks. Within two hours, the wines worthy of being submitted to the regional merchants had been selected. The time had not yet come for white or rosé wines, for which there was no demand and for which vinification techniques were still rudimentary.

Once the session was over, the best bottles were displayed in the dining room. We would then progress to the next stage of tasting, moving from purely mechanical and olfactory criteria to that of feeling and experience. When you eat, drinking wine takes on its full meaning and takes the wine even further. For example, a chemical reaction, described by the oenologist Pierre Casamayor, brings together the proteins and the marble of the meat with red wine tannins. This is when you truly resonate with the wine, understanding its full potential and complex structure.

The tastevin was used in the laboratory and ISO* glasses would be set on the table. I was ten when my father invited me to join him for my first wine tasting session, on a Wednesday after school. I was proud, a little bit in awe, and impatient to contribute comments. To be honest, what excited me most was the energetic spitting, which allowed me to reach the spittoon from two metres away, thanks to a simultaneous pinching of the tongue and a powerful breath of air. I quickly developed my own technique so that I could be judged trustworthy. In terms of sensations and tasting notes, I'd have to wait a while. It became a ritual. Every Wednesday, I took part in these timeless moments that I eagerly

* International Standards Organisation or ISO wine glasses are recognised internationally as the standard design for tasting. The rounded bowl and narrow sides allow the wine to be swirled easily without any spillage. The rim helps contain all the delightful aromas and enhances appreciation.

awaited. I was happy and would ask questions about geography – where are Castelmaure, Caramany, Minerve, areas distant from my home village? Very early, I understood the meaning of the grandeur of terroirs and their unique expression.

Tasting the wines was the first step. The second one, definitely the most important one, was blending them. To taste the base wines, score them, understand their personality and their potential and from there build a structure, which, like a team, would give birth to a collective expression, greater than the strength of each individual. My father Georges, trained by Henri Demolombe and Jean-Henri Dubernet, two wise figures in the world of wine, was gifted with this clairvoyant ability, and took a constantly renewed sensual pleasure in magnifying terroirs and injecting soul into an estate wine or a cuvée. The approach was empirical even if the science of oenology was in its early days. Physical and chemical analysis were used as safeguards and as validation of a job well done. Blending a table wine, an IGP wine or a cru wine doesn't require the same precision but demands the same level of commitment.

Rituals

Blending wine is an alchemy, an expression of the human spirit, a pathway that allows elements to align and enable their sublimation. The blending process is the cornerstone of successful winemaking. To magnify a vintage means understanding its essence and then revealing its personality. The first stage is timeless, linked to terroir and the spirit of the place; the second

Blending wine is an alchemy, an expression of the human spirit, a pathway that allows ingredients to align and enables their sublimation.

hinges on human work during the vine cycle and the vagaries of weather from flowering to the harvest. Choosing the harvest date, rather than being subjected to it, is a defining element for the life of the wine and its hierarchy in the rankings of vintages. There is no perfect blend, but there can be a perfect balance. All the previous stages are important: pruning the vines, which regenerate from December to March, then grow new shoots, and bud in spring before grapes appear. I love the vine in bloom during the month of May. It is a fleeting time, fragrant and fragile. When grapes appear and clusters are neither too tight, nor too loose, the countdown starts: one hundred days to harvest. *Véraison**, at the end of July, brings us closer to picking and the harvest feast. Many winegrowers make token offerings to Dionysus to protect the harvest.

The harvest date must be chosen, not being subjected to. If my vineyard work and daily toil have met the demands of the vintage, my teams and I can choose the best timing to bring in the grapes and minimise risks linked to the year's vagaries.

Grapes for white wine are mostly picked and put into tanks earlier than reds to preserve freshness and acidity. Picking red grapes involves greater risk-taking, which ultimately differentiates between good and great wines. Roaming the

---

* Véraison represents the transition from berry growth to berry ripening when the grapes change colour.

vineyards from top to bottom and across the hills, tasting the grapes, crunching the pips between one's teeth all require endurance, discipline, and the ability to spot the tipping point, the ideal timing to harvest the plot when the grapes are at their very best in terms of maturity. Once in the vat, or the press for whites and rosés, most of the yearly cycle is over.

'Fermentation acts as an aroma enhancer and releases the aromatic compounds of the grape, so that the juice produces more of an aroma than the grape itself,' said Émile Peynaud, the oenologist. Humility is required at this stage as it would be presumptuous to believe one is in control. When the condition of the grapes is healthy in good years, or after selection in difficult years, I can savour that magical moment when the cellar fills with hundreds of millions of yeasts that turn sugar into alcohol and deliver the true identity of the vintage. This stage, lasting between eight and fifteen days, belongs to the universe. Our cellarmasters check temperatures and aerate the grape must, while taking care to moisten the cap for three to five minutes per day. 'Managing macerations can be intuitive but managing fermentations requires oenological knowledge,' said the expert Denis Dubourdieu. The winegrower oversees the process, and the expert marks out the way ahead.

All these stages, punctuated by the four seasons, and their outcome at the beginning of autumn, are essential but not quite enough to create a great wine. There are no magicians in wine cellars. Our work is to pick healthy ripe grapes. The work of the oenologist may sometimes turn lost causes into quality wine, as experience and technical know-how can win ill-fated battles despite all odds. In no case will there be a miracle; the quintessence can only be the culmination of a succession of successful steps, an alchemy of ripe and healthy grapes picked in limited quantity and at the exact right time. All these steps, followed by a careful vinification and fining of the winter grape musts prepare them for the moment of truth. This preparatory work is indispensable and represents the fertile compost needed for the ultimate experience. Nature, at this point, leaves us to do our meticulous work which will sometimes create a masterpiece.

There is a hierarchy in wine quality. Beyond the prestige of a country, region or appellation, the aromas and flavours of the wine vary between good, very good, excellent, and exceptional. A good wine is a wine for daily consumption; faithful to its origins, it keeps its promise of taste. It reflects its terroir and meets consumers' expectations. As soon as we enter the category of very good wines, we change dimension. We go from taste to what is after-taste. The mid-palate offers a taut texture, complexity, and depth, taking over your palate. This is the domain of the wine connoisseurs. Excellence is the path to follow and my goal is to satisfy the seekers of rare emotions. An exceptional wine rises above human genius. It is the result of a perfect climatic sequence that creates a legendary vintage. The upper three levels of satisfaction - very good, excellent, and exceptional - will only be revealed with caution, experience, virtuosity, know-how, and the touch of madness that conditions the final blend.

Sometimes it is more difficult to make good wine than great wine, as consistency and typicity, especially for branded wines produced in large volumes, are never easy to guarantee.

To produce a very good wine from a great terroir is a missed opportunity, as expectations should match the reputation of the estate. Creating a successful blend is a hazardous venture that requires asceticism, humility, and time, from August when the decision to harvest is taken to the finalisation of the blend three to four months later.

I immerse myself in the vintage, my brain absorbing tons of data, often without conscious awareness, while specific emotions stir in my heart, influencing me at the decisive moment.

Walking in the vineyards, tasting the grapes, conversing with the team, observing the surrounding nature and biotope, and touching the soils, several times in each plot over forty days, are the basic principles I adhere to every year. I immerse myself in the vintage, my brain absorbing tons of data, often without conscious awareness, while specific emotions stir in my heart, influencing me at the decisive moment. I metaphorically don my blending attire and embark on the introspection process. I absorb the sensations that will inform my tasting sessions. It is extremely rare to achieve the expected results on the first attempt. Patience to progress slowly, step by step, stage by stage, is essential, as is the willingness to err in order to discover the guiding principle close to our hearts. Preparing for excellence is akin to preparing for a great rugby match; a good night's sleep, a light meal the night before, and emotional stability are prerequisites.

Asceticism

The room, or rather the sanctuary, as thousands of blending hours have already been spent there, has been prepared. The samples have been readied, the lighting adjusted to the desired level, and the temperature brought to fourteen degrees Celsius for white and rosé wines, and sixteen degrees Celsius for red wines. Before I begin, I remind my team of the vintage specificities, say a few words and boost the group's energy by recalling the objectives to be achieved. Most of the time, I know within half an hour if the day is auspicious for emotional and sensuous transcendence. It may happen that my palate, my receptacle for taste, perceives too much astringency or bitterness and isn't in sync with the profile of the wines. In that case, it is best to have the intelligence and humility to withdraw and postpone the work to be done. Excellence necessitates a symbiosis between team members, fostering rising excitement and a different state of vibration. We enter a form of heightened sensitivity that enables us to capture all external information.

Letting go is the trickiest moment, freeing my creative potential and intuitions to find the sublime proportion. There are no predefined principles imposing specific percentages of the product of each plot in the final blend. While there are set rules and specificities for appellations, they thankfully leave a lot of flexibility to ensure each vintage is a unique piece. The basic premise is that blending the best vats will never create the best wine. One must seek the blend that creates a link and enhances complementarities. It can become an obsession, as achieving the required musicality on the first try is not common. Experience, in this case, is a decisive tool that, by reminding us of past sessions, will guide us toward the truth.

When we achieve the perfect balance, I know it. I feel it. I am moved by this profound pleasure shared with the team that arises from creating a masterpiece.

Compromise on the path to excellence is not an option. It may be suggested and agreed upon when the vintage is not great and ambitious goals are revised downward. When we achieve the perfect balance, I know it. I feel it. I am moved by this profound pleasure shared with the team that arises from creating a masterpiece. It is an ecstatic moment, a complete achievement, and a revelation.

At the end of the blending session, I take a bottle of the nectar to the restaurant. Tasting without drinking is an exercise that requires proven qualities but tasting while drinking is another experience altogether. I create conditions for sharing within the team around a convivial meal, and with animal proteins if red wine is served.

This experience validates the first step and allows moving on to the actual blending in the cellar, followed by the transfer to the barrels. This shared meal is also a special moment, an intimate celebration that marks the culmination of fifteen months of work and opens the third phase of barrel maturation. This twelve-month sequence represents a complete cycle in itself that allows wine, through a managed oxidation process, to evolve patiently along with the seasons and prepare for bottling. The spring and autumn equinoxes are important dates in the evolution of wine. Wine is alive; it senses change and the rhythm of the seasons. The colour evolves, tannins soften, the length develops, complexity increases, the percentage of new oak having been determined by the wine structure and the sum of temperatures of the past year. In the last ten years climate change has been degrading grape tannins. Therefore, we have toned down our use of new barrels to preserve the fruit and the taste of terroir.

The identity of an excellent wine is a subtle alliance between climate, grape varieties, terroir, and the human being who has revealed it with full consciousness. This kind of behaviour and this desire to explore new pathways isn't the same as academic knowledge. It is more akin to the path of initiation that marks every stage of my life, as I am simultaneously curious, determined, and resolved to live timeless experiences.

Once arrived in our 'holy of holies,' we close the door, turn off our phones, and do not set a time limit. A session can last three or five hours, as long as energy is present, and tastebuds are receptive. For very tannic wines, the session is shortened as not enough saliva is produced to moisten the mouth and wine starts to burn the inside of the cheeks.

The blending work at that level

The blending work at that level mobilises the physical and emotional bodies, mind and spirit. The perfect harmony is the result of a multidimensional approach. Man transcends matter and reaches a vibrational level akin to the sacred.

mobilises the physical and emotional bodies, mind and spirit. The perfect harmony is the result of a multidimensional approach. Man transcends matter and reaches a vibrational level akin to the sacred.

Wine is a binder that warms people's hearts and brings them together. In many religions, it symbolises celebration, and in Christianity, it symbolises the blood of Christ. This spiritual dimension enhances clairvoyance, improves perception, reveals intuitions and provides dazzling insights that open the doors to wine heaven. In Mediterranean countries, wine has always been part of pagan and religious rituals. It is sanctified in temples and celebrated in cities. The monks of the Abbey of Notre-Dame de Cîteaux and of the Abbey of Cluny revealed Burgundy and named the terroirs – recently renamed 'climats' – of this magical region, now registered as UNESCO World Heritage Sites. Clerics understood the spirit of wine. Across France, Spain, Italy, Portugal, Greece, as well as in Lebanon, Israel, and elsewhere, hillsides were planted with vines. No other drink can quench your thirst, lift your spirits and gladden the hearts of men and women simultaneously. Inebriation is another form of joy. It creates a social bond and drives existential anxieties away.

This spiritual dimension enhances clairvoyance, improves perception, reveals intuitions and provides dazzling insights that open the doors to wine heaven.

The ceremony dedicated to great wines, those that reveal the treasures and secrets of the terroir, deserves particular attention.

A degree of education is required to resonate with the soul of wine. The most important thing is to choose the right guests, and then the food. The selected vintage should have reached an initial stage of maturity. Ten years of bottle age is a good start. Opening the bottle one to two hours before the meal allows for a light and gentle aeration of the wine. If the wine tastes good, it doesn't need to be decanted. The selection of the right glasses is more important than many people think. The shape, height, thinness of the goblet, and its opening all play a role in enhancing pleasure. I never tire of looking at the faces around the table and how they light up when the wine reveals its secrets. Some will recognise the sublime expression of a divine nectar before others. An unexpected moment of sharing sometimes occurs when the communion of spirits takes over the table and everyone becomes individually and collectively aware of this moment of grace. Emotion is at its highest, and the message is so potent that words are unnecessary. This deep joy makes the meal sacred and encourages open-heartedness.

Blending made me understand the responsibility that comes with the creation of the new vintage. One must be ready to meet history, cultivate the constant search for excellence, and prepare hearts to welcome these timeless moments. One will never know the final destination of the bottles one produces. Very few will be drunk at the apex of their maturity, with the right serving ritual and necessary preparation. But if only one table of diners celebrates one wine at the optimal moment in the best company, the spark will ignite the group and never die.

Legendary wines

The story of wine is made up of magical moments when gravity is suspended, and that can leave a lasting impression on one's life. When drinking a legendary wine, there is no surprise effect but rather an expectation of an exceptional experience. Drinking a bottle of Romanée-Conti 1961 or Château-Latour 1961 – perhaps the two best wines in the world – is today a privilege reserved for the very wealthy few and those lucky enough to already have such bottles in their cellar. I have been lucky to drink these legendary wines in very good company. It is rather difficult in such moments to break away from conventions and trite discourse, as the loss of gravity is so powerful that it destroys any attempt to wax lyrical. I can, however, confirm that the balance, harmony, breeding, elegance, depth, and soul of these two wines still inhabit my head and my heart. Olfactory memory is indelible. When I taste a great wine for the second time, I am overwhelmed by all the memories that rise to the surface and remind me of the exact time, place, food, and people that accompanied my first experience.

In November 2021, I was invited to Burgundy to commemorate the tenth anniversary of the death of Patrick Collomb, a chartered accountant who was also a very dear friend, confidant and advisor. Aubert de Villaine, the Faiveley and Boisset families, and I had one thing in common: the same advisor. He was much more than that: he was the incarnation of the warrior monk, always available and of scintillating intelligence. His considerable help in the 2000s in consolidating my business, with his faithful

Arnaud Chanteranne and Silvère Patriat, taking the right legal decisions, and reassuring my financial backers, was invaluable. He was also a lover of great wines. At his commemorative luncheon, we drank all the great Burgundy wines. I have always been a fan of this region and its terroirs, and I have a particular affection for the winegrowers who have a strategic approach to the management of their different parcels. Each winegrower oversees their own destiny. They must write their own scoresheet with the raw material at their disposal and get the very best out of their plots. Revealing the true expression of a plot is more like a monk's work than expressing the quintessence of several grape varieties spread over several plots: the soul of the terroir or the soul of the estate. A vineyard plot is the essence of nature magnified by the precision of the winegrower's skill. A château is a succession of micro terroirs to be blended, put to music, and allowed to vibrate. It is interesting for the enlightened wine drinker to understand these two different ways towards excellence.

Each winegrower oversees their own destiny. They must write their own scoresheet with the raw material at their disposal and get the very best out of their plots.

Aubert de Villaine is Burgundy's living legend. He lives and breathes the identity of the region. He is the guardian of the temple and a guide for all winemakers searching for the absolute. At the end of this lunch, he surprised us with a magnum of La Tâche 1990. The meal was already one of my most memorable before this divine nectar introduced us to another dimension, both terrestrial and celestial. The breath of the Holy Spirit descended upon the room, and we drank a last toast to our dearly beloved friend. There are wines and sometimes vintages that possess a fullness symbolised by a unique character, a balance, and a harmony between verticality and depth. This type of experience made me want to develop my own plot selection - La Forge, Le Viala, L'Hospitalitas, L'Aigle Royal, and more recently Plantabelle -to experience this need for the absolute and the ultimate and deliberate simplicity at the expense of creative blending. Having several estates allows me to reinvent myself and explore different pathways towards the nirvana of wine.

Family

The bedrock of my ambition and success rests on solid foundations: a loving yet demanding upbringing and a resilient family. Viticulture has always been the common denominator of the Bertrand family.

Languedoc monoculture at the beginning of the 20th century fed my family. My grandmother Paule, my uncles, and aunts used to live by the rhythm of the seasons, from pruning to flowering, *véraison*, and harvest. The cooperative cellars of each village enabled the pooling of resources from all the local winemaking estates, rallied energies, and alleviated suffering. These so-called *vins de misère* or misery wines, would quench the thirst of rural populations and industrial France in the first decades of the last century.

This cooperative experience was fertile ground for French

socialism, highlighting class wars and fighting against the bourgeoisie. Jean Jaurès and Léon Blum hailed from the South of France, one from the Tarn department, the other from the Aude, and both embodied its spirit. Later, General de Gaulle brought forth a new vision for our country and restored hope and ambition while promoting a social and human form of capitalism. Two visions of politics but one France that works, moves forward, and fights for popular and identity-based values.

The concept of France as a country was created by Charlemagne and Saint Louis, the medieval king, and shaped later by the Age of Enlightenment. Together, they built the French spirit and its genius for art and literature, agriculture, and the diversity of terroirs and territories. I've always felt the strength of this country, admired its landscapes, and felt at one with this identity that fed the hopes and dreams of several generations and created a social model that is a bedrock of community cohesion. Times have changed. Europe strengthened the links between nations after the Second World War, widened horizons and fraternity between peoples, and developed the economic relations that have fostered growth for over 40 years.

French viticulture benefited from this development. It inspired the European continent, the USA, and then the world. Our country's gastronomy, faithful to the genius of Escoffier, transcended all our grandmothers' recipes and ennobled the French lifestyle. The Bertrand family tradition was no exception. Sunday lunch took on a new dimension as it defined the weekly day of rest. After morning mass and, for some, a pitstop at the local bar for a vermouth or a pastis, it was time for lunch. At twelve noon, everybody was sitting around the table. The procession of ancestral know-how could start. The ritual never changed. Setting the table would bring together plates gifted on the occasion of our grandparents' wedding, and the silver cutlery was brought out. Crystal glasses added a very specific French touch. Dishes followed one another. Local cold cuts would get the proceedings started, mimosa eggs would follow, a duck liver salad would introduce the arrival of a fish in sauce, and a cut of beef would precede a poultry dish. Cheese would herald the arrival of puddings, often an *île flottante*. The wines of the estate would be served with all these dishes, cooked by my grandmother. This was in the seventies, and it was important to celebrate and honour guests. And, for this generation that lived through war, famine, and misery, also to compensate with opulence and the art of entertainment. Food was then the biggest household expense. People would entertain and loved spending time together. The Sunday lunch ritual is still part of my lifestyle even though I limit myself to three or four food and wine matches.

I've kept this love of food, and this desire for sharing, inherited from my grandmother and my parents. My sister Guylaine is also imbued with these values. When my wife Ingrid arrived in my village of Saint André de Roquelongue, her Provençal upbringing soon adapted to the Occitan lifestyle.

She was able to adjust to rural life and win over my family and my loved ones. She has been a support for me as well as a generous soul who stimulates me. The strength of our love helped us to overcome hurdles and see further ahead. She has encouraged me to take risks and to go and conquer the world. Ingrid has a very developed intuition and an emotional ease that enables a holistic approach to her work as a healer. I introduced her to the world of wine, its secrets, and customs. Our children, Emma and Mathias, have been brought up within this family tradition, which is a bedrock and an anchor. In turn, Emma and Mathias have developed the fine palates needed to be the first people to enjoy the blends of Cigalus, Villemajou or La Forge and endorse the quality of the vintage. Our children have grown surrounded by love and immersed in the sharing values and the demands of the agricultural environment where everything must be deserved and earned.

Fundamentals are in place, and family spirit guarantees a template, a long-term vision, and an agility able to meet the demands and the complexity of the modern world.

Carpe Diem.

Multidimensional Opening

The evolution of humanity has favoured the development of humankind and its leading position on Earth. In less than two hundred years, we have progressed from satisfying basic needs to enjoying unparalleled life comforts, albeit at different levels across countries and continents. The development of international exchanges, diplomacy, philosophy, culture, and art has fostered wine consumption, the refinement of gastronomy, and the multiplication of experiences. France represents the quintessence of a lifestyle where wine plays a major role.

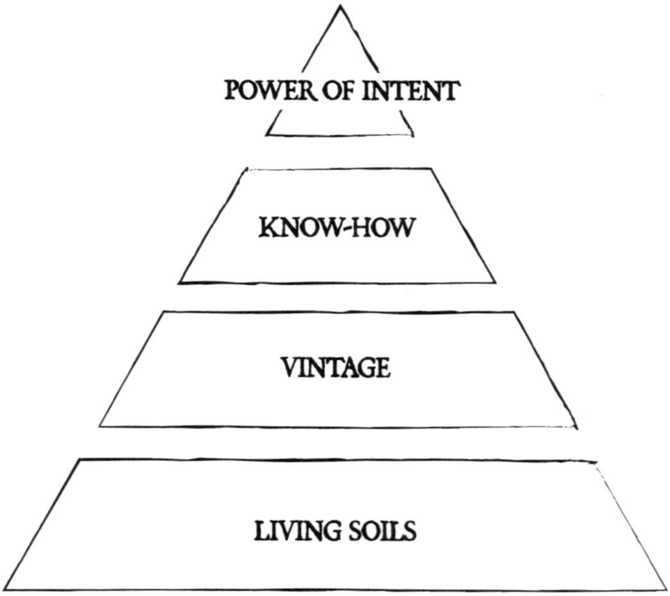

* MULTIDIMENSIONAL PYRAMID *

Winegrowers are farmers when they look after landscapes, local rivers, and care for biodiversity. They become craftsmen when they apply advanced principles to foster a quest for excellence in the service of a refined wine with a strong identity. Those who dare to take it further turn into artists. They develop a heightened sensitivity and a deep connection with their vineyard, paired with a requirement for high standards, strength, and passion for their craft, symbolic of their deep commitment. This spiritual quest opens the door to multidimensional wine, able to transcend and reveal the soul of wine.

A living soil guarantees substantial microbial activity and the plant's capacity to draw strength and energy from its surroundings and feel the rhythm of the seasons.

The interaction between earthly and celestial forces depends on the quality of the soils. A living soil guarantees substantial microbial activity and the plant's capacity to draw strength and energy from its surroundings and feel the rhythm of the seasons. Microorganisms, bacteria, and fungi create a favourable environment for the needs of the vine, magnified by biodynamic viticulture. It is the same for agriculture.

Understanding the living world was part of Greek philosophy. Aristotle understood it. Much later, in 1796, Sir Samuel Hahnemann conceptualised this natural approach using plants to help with human health. He created homeopathy, an alternative therapy based on the individualisation of patients, identification of symptoms, and matching treatments, different from one person to another. The dilution methods he applied allow curing a patient with a substance that would emulate their symptoms if it were concentrated. After suffering from serious liver issues, I tried conventional treatments in the 90s that didn't improve my condition. On the recommendation of my friend Jean Claude Berrouet, I met François Mazel, a remarkable homeopath who identified and cured my pains in a few weeks. The advantage of this type of treatment rests on seeking solutions to the root of the problem and not its consequence. It allowed me to better understand the complexity of human beings, their interactions, and the influence of plants on human health.

In 1790, Goethe published a major scientific work, 'Metamorphosis of Plants'. He was the first to understand and reveal how geology, mineralogy and botany function, fostering a better understanding of nature. This philanthropic and visionary genius influenced the world of art, sciences, philosophy, and politics. His works influenced Rudolf Steiner's, and in 1924, during eight conferences, Steiner established the basics of biodynamic principles, used mainly in agriculture and, more recently, in viticulture by pioneers like François Bouchet and Nicolas Joly. Biodynamic principles are homeopathy for plants by plants. Maria Thun later invented the lunar calendar and identified the flower, fruit, leaf, and root days, as well as lunar nodes, to help the agricultural world optimise biodynamic practices. Biodynamic preparations are mainly made of plants such as yarrow, dandelion, or nettle. Silica and cow dung are also used. All these ingredients are blended with potentised water and sprayed according to the astral calendar.

Humankind feels the forces of the universe and belongs to a harmonious and infinite structure. The human spirit can visualise a transcended representation of matter and thus create a new dimension fostering the balance of ecosystems. Plants obey the same forces and rhythms. Cycles are immutable and follow principles that developed life on Earth. Steiner inspired Ehrenfried Pfeiffer, who went on to invent copper chloride crystallisation in 1925, a way to assess the energetic quality of a product. Copper chloride crystallisation reveals differences in quality and energy in wine, grapes, shoots, or leaves samples. Each stage was validated scientifically and has been followed by standardisation processes such as ISO 9000 in Germany in the 2010s.

These principles inform the life of our vineyards and our wines throughout the year. During the winter, we monitor the activity and efficiency of the vines' rooting, as well as their interactions with the soil and subsoil, the latter of which has an impact on the next vintage. During the spring, we check if the plant development is in phase with its physiological cycle to anticipate a possible maturity lag at the end of the cycle. We also observe the flow potentials of raw and processed sap. Ahead of the harvest, we choose the optimal date to start picking according to the aromatic profiles desired for each wine. In the cellar, from the moment when grape musts start fermenting, until blending, we collect useful information for the smooth running of the process and the coherence of the blending of the vats. All this data will determine the signature of the vintage, its energetic potential, the link with the terroir, and the longevity of the wines. This information will assist in constructing the architecture of the wine, the birth of its character and its identity.

Our ancestors had the wisdom, humility, and intuition to use only natural products to work their vines and soils. Their empirical knowledge was built up and passed down through generations in the vineyard and the cellar. Lunar cycles were studied carefully. The 1945 and 1961 vintages were exceptional, and 1947, 1949, 1953, 1959, and 1975 were excellent. All these vintages were made before the invention of synthetic chemistry, which has indeed contributed to protecting the volumes harvested but also negatively impacted the life of the soils and standardised the taste of wine.

Great vintages offer the perfect conditions for viticultural and oenological know-how to align and create memorable wines that will stand the test of time and weather decades of ageing. A strong will, allied with mindfulness, fosters the creation of a masterpiece that offers a unique feeling and vibration. The power of the intent of the winegrower, their understanding of ecosystems, the spiritual dimension, and emotional intelligence create the necessary conditions for this unique experience.

The power of the intent of the winegrower, their understanding of ecosystems, the spiritual dimension, and emotional intelligence create the necessary conditions for this unique experience.

Terroir

That impossible-to-translate French word describes a limited geographical area, its environmental factors and how they impact agricultural production. It differs from the notion of territory, which encompasses several terroirs, areas, and conurbations. Viticultural terroirs express heritage, uphold traditions, and clamour for Appellations and Protected Geographical Indications. They are a refined expression of geography, history, geology, topography, and climates. They constitute a framework that, from generation to generation, will evolve slowly with the blessing of the National Institute of Origin and Quality (INAO). The physicochemical structure of a soil, such as limestone, silica, granite, volcanic soil, clay, and sand, goes towards describing it. The choice of grape varieties offers the expected typicity and taste, guarding this viticultural identity as long as the winegrower understands its origin, wants it, and seeks the quality it represents. This is an individual approach that will sublimate the collective spirit of an area.

The internationalisation of the wine trade, the standardisation of production rules and oenological processes, and the varietal wines system promoted by the New World have hugely challenged the hegemony of the European viticultural organisation model. The economic power and marketing strength of the large Australian and American groups, who often also produce spirits, beers, or ready-to-drink beverages (RTDs), have sped up the rhythm of the supply chain represented by importers, distributors, and hospitality.

The average quality of wine has never been higher, and enjoyment is guaranteed. The future of terroir wines is conditional on quality improvement and a guarantee that will match wine drinkers' expectations. The challenge is real and spares no one. Bordeaux, whose top wines achieve record price levels, is going through a deep crisis, caused by overproduction and failing sales of generic wines. Sales of red Rhône wines are also declining. Languedoc offers a mix of varietal and terroir wines of different colours, giving the region more flexibility to adjust to this changing environment without any complacency. We now operate in a very competitive environment dictated by marketing and market rules, not always compatible with the world of wine.

Terroir wines must reinvent themselves and reveal 'the taste of somewhere' rather than just 'the taste of something'. The second half of the game between terroir and varietal wines is kicking off. It is tricky for viticulture, a multigenerational business in which products are sometimes created years before they are consumed, to meet market expectations. Solving the complex equation between long-term vision and short-term answers requires flexibility and adaptability. The good news is that the whole world still wants to drink wine and include it in its gastronomic and social rituals.

Prestige wines have adopted the codes of accessible luxury, and auctions of rare bottles help to reinforce the image of our regions. The surge in demand for Champagne and the resulting price increases after the Covid crisis respond to growing international needs and sanctify the star liquid of our industry. The genius of that region is to have erased the notion of vintage and highlighted the *grandes maisons*, turning them over centuries into powerful and world-famous brands. It's an opportunity for France and a unique example of industry structure.

Market balance, range segmentation, terroir hierarchy, and controlled marketing are prerequisites to eventually sharing added value. When a denomination turns into a brand, it generates lasting success. The reputation of regions, illustrated by the rising demand for Burgundy wines, is different and has more to do with tradition, carried on by family companies of winegrowers or merchants.

Each region must find its template and test it over time. The Northern Rhône has emulated its northern neighbour Burgundy, with a referent grape variety, Syrah; well-identified terroirs; iconic plots and winemakers; precise work; and biodynamic agriculture more often than not, as well as the proximity of a gastronomic city. The Southern Rhône, and especially Châteauneuf-du-Pape, praises diversity with thirteen grape varieties without any limits, the epitome of absolute liberalism.

Taste Identity

Bordeaux initially, but also Provence, champions blending grape varieties. Languedoc, with its Greco-Roman heritage and vast area, develops segmentation and hierarchisation in the service of independent growers, merchants, and cooperatives. In the South of France, between the River Rhône and Spain, we sit at a strategic crossroads and face our destiny. Two thousand four hundred years ago, Greek settlers arrived in the ancient city of Agde, bringing with them amphorae and vine stocks, including Clairette. For centuries, this grape variety produced the only local white wine. It has now become the pride of winegrowers from the village of Adissan. Clairette has retained the same taste identity because its genome hasn't changed in twenty-four centuries. Drinking this wine evokes the message of the Greek poet Alcaeus, later echoed by Pliny the Elder: *'In vino veritas'.*

Greeks, Romans, Visigoths, and Cathars have all contributed to building up the Languedoc, giving it a social and spiritual dimension. The confirmation of a true territorial identity and taste emerged later, at the beginning of the 1960s. The recent quality increase in the viticultural South of France, sometimes called Occitania, is impressive and the result of a specific farming and winegrowing culture. For a long time, excellence was an impossibility against a background of infighting among the leaders of viticultural affairs. The legacy of Marcelin Albert, a French café owner and winegrower considered the leader of the 1907 revolt of the Languedoc winegrowers, carried with it the marks of a type of standardisation. The unchallenged domination of the Béziers rugby team between 1961 and 1984 symbolised this era. Béziers, a Cathar citadel that never surrendered and whose last remaining heretics were burned at the stake, reflects the incredible violence and tragedy of these people. During the thirteenth century, they heralded and preached a different form of Christianity, closer to nature, generating a shockwave that shook the region for centuries. Béziers was also the worldwide capital city of table wine, one of the main trading places where trainloads of standard 10-, 11-, or 12-degree wine were shipped all over France.

Narbonne, known as Narbo Martius in Roman times and located between Carcassonne, Béziers, and Albi, had a different influence. It was the first Roman settlement in Gaul, established in 118 BC. The Narbonensis empire stretched from Toledo to the Alps, with its influence lasting for several centuries. Just as Mars, from whom the name Martius is derived (meaning sacred to Mars, martial), was a warrior god, Narbonne is a town that has always had the strength to claim its territory, identity, and choices. In the 1970s to the 1990s, epic battles between the two rugby teams—Béziers fielding Estève, Palmier, Astre, and Vaquerin, and Narbonne with Spanghero, Maso, Sangali, and Codorniou—celebrated those sporting heroes. After the matches, people would indulge in wine and food to celebrate victories and forget defeats.

The production of the terroirs of Saint-Chinian and Faugères, and Corbières, Fitou, and Minervois, began to introduce consumers to a different taste identity and establish it as a new reality. The South of France, a twenty-year-old denomination used to locate and identify our large region, presents a clear and diversified offer: on one hand, Languedoc and Roussillon wines, and, on the other, Oc varietal wines. This is an opportunity to structure such a large region with a diversity of terroirs, climates, and heritage. After seeing the emergence of terroir selection initiated by the chambers of agriculture and the rise of varietal wines with Jacques Gravegeal and Robert Skalli, some iconoclastic winegrowers like Aimé Guibert; the Jeanjean brothers; the Dauré, Laboucarié, and Bergès families; Marlène Soria; Georges Bertrand; and a few others, challenged the received order and chose to assert the identity of their estates. Initially, this was done in a solitary and ambitious way, but by the 1980s, there was legitimate recognition of their terroir.

My task and that of my teams has been to take this approach in the vineyards even further through the introduction of biodynamics. This technique stimulates plants, revives soils, and delivers a more complex and authentic wine expression. The plot selection of high-quality grapes, hand-harvested, takes us to another dimension. When the right conditions are brought together, and the will of men and women demands progress, it becomes possible to create great wines. I've always had a clear vision that my beloved region had the potential to rival the best wines in the world while affirming its differences and personality.

Villemajou, Cigalus et La Livinière

The Villemajou estate represents the benchmark, my father's history, and the family's heritage. The road is mapped out for me. I continue the work accomplished by Georges over twenty-five years and maintain the terroir taste he knew so well how to reveal. Jean Algrain, the lead climber, and now Christophe Sournies and his faithful team continue the family tradition.

Purchasing other estates answered the need to discover new horizons, tied to the visceral need to create something new. Starting with a blank or almost blank sheet of paper has always been my credo. The common denominator in my purchasing choices is terroir, the only constant in a winegrowing estate. One can choose a new team, plant new grape varieties, and update the cellar, but it's impossible to change the soil and the subsoil.

The common denominator in my purchasing choices is terroir, the only constant in a winegrowing estate. One can choose a new team, plant new grape varieties, and update the cellar, but it's impossible to change the soil and the subsoil.

My first acquisition, the La Clause estate, renamed Cigalus, answered the need to leave the village of my childhood, Saint-André de Roquelongue, and to free myself from designations of origin. The diversity of the grape varieties planted by the previous owner offered an opening and allowed me to imagine, thanks to a high-quality clay and limestone soil, a blend of local and international grape varieties. It's a challenge that Bertrand Boileau and Laurent Monnerris managed to take up. I settled at the estate with my wife, Ingrid, and we enlarged the house when Emma was born in 1998 and Mathias in 2000. The family adventure continued near the family birthplace.

In 1997, the purchase of the Château Laville Bertrou in La Livinière answered different criteria. The foothills of the Black Mountain are split into two parts: the terraces and the plateau called the Causse. Below, fertile and well-drained soils favour the development of Syrah, and, in the foothills, limestone soils ensure the freshness of the Carignan and Grenache grape varieties. Guy

Baldo contributed to establishing the credentials of this estate.

The beauty of the landscapes around La Livinière and its natural ecosystem have fed my vision and inspired me to create Clos d'Ora in the surrounding hills. Five hectares of *garrigue* separated a very old plot of Carignan and a thirty-year-old plot of Syrah. On the top of the hill, a very old sheepfold demolished during the Second World War was waiting to be revived. The northern wind blows in the evening and keeps the summer nights fresh, protecting the grapes' aromatic potential. La Livinière is the kingdom of the Syrah grape variety in Languedoc, and Clos d'Ora became, over ten years, a novel experiment. On top of a geological fault, an area of contact between limestones and marls magnifies connections between earth and heaven. The feeling it creates is rather surprising. The peace, love, and harmony exuded by this extraordinary site connect us with the divine.

Ora conveys the idea of prayer in Latin and time in the future in Greek. The strength of intention opened a field of possibilities on this plot, making our task fascinating and exhilarating. Olivier Nollevalle understood its meaning. Over ten vintages, he knew how to represent the message of the Clos and bring out the best in the teams in the quest for excellence, while producing an exceptional wine.

Château l'Hospitalet, Domaine de l'Aigle, Château La Sauvageonne and Château Aigues Vives

The story of Château l'Hospitalet began in 2002 when I acquired it from Jacques Ribourel, who had renovated the estate in the

1990s, making it one of the first oenotourism sites in France. Ribourel successfully combined wine and gastronomy, offering a visitor's experience ahead of its time. I chose to expand on it by adding culture and music to celebrate the Mediterranean lifestyle. The architecture and perspectives of the estate perfectly embody the revival of our region. However, it needed a new soul, one that affirmed its Languedoc personality. Transforming it into the flagship estate for the La Clape denomination within the Narbonne natural park was key, as was the drive for excellence shared with Marc Olivier Trompette, the vineyard manager. The hard limestone terroir was waiting to be revealed. The old vines and the elimination of chemical products have allowed this terroir to express its full potential. These soils, which are poor and do not retain water, rely on crucial August rains to complete the vines' maturity cycle, resulting in wines with minerality, freshness, fruit, and tension. Good vintages travel far, perfectly encapsulating the saying 'an iron fist in a velvet glove' for the red blend of Syrah, Grenache, and Mourvèdre. The white blend, combining Bourboulenc, Grenache, Rolle, and Viognier, is also characterful. We have further expanded our holdings in La Clape with the acquisition of the Karantes and Tarailhan vineyards.

Château l'Hospitalet is sold worldwide, with the 2017 vintage being selected as the best red wine at the International Wine Challenge in London. This wine also celebrated the alliance between France and China, symbolising the friendship between the French and Chinese presidents during a French presidential visit to Shanghai in 2019. Great wines delight the hearts of people and can also serve as valuable allies in international diplomacy,

Great wines delight the hearts of people and can also serve as valuable allies in international diplomacy, representing a universal symbol of fraternity and offering a unique opportunity to elevate official debates with an allegorical touch.

representing a universal symbol of fraternity and offering a unique opportunity to elevate official debates with an allegorical touch. Wine, like music, can transport us to different levels of resonance with the universe, creating inspiring moments.

One day in 2006, while driving towards Limoux, I turned towards Roquetaillade, a mountain village set in the middle of a natural amphitheatre open in four directions. The Domaine de l'Aigle, created by Jean-Louis Denois, captivated me. Originally from Champagne, Denois recognised the potential of this high-altitude terroir for sparkling wines as well as premium Chardonnay and Pinot Noir. He sold the estate to Antonin Rodet, a Burgundian company that expanded the vineyard. Bertrand de Villars, with his knowledge and passion, cultivated the 40 hectares and built a new cellar from local stones. However, a change in company governance halted his progress. My first visit to the estate was inspiring. The village was picturesque. The natural slopes, quality vegetal material, and well-exposed clay-limestone terroir guaranteed Chardonnay's freshness and Pinot Noir's maturity. The staff was talented but seemed stuck in time. Wanting to make the most of the approaching harvest, I quickly arranged an agreement with the shareholder, signed at the end of August, and began harvesting. It took me three years to understand the optimal picking date for Pinot Noir, a grape variety that fascinates me with its elegance and power. The estate quickly achieved commercial success, and Thibaut Haentjens and his team continue the Limoux winegrowing tradition.

In 2012, Vignoble et Investissements contacted me about Château La Sauvageonne. Although I was unfamiliar with the area, Michel Veyrié, the estate agent, convinced me with his description. I arrived at the end of the afternoon and met Antoine Cotes, the estate manager for almost twenty years. He pointed out the outlines of the property and explained the schist and '*ruffes*' (volcanic soil) terroir. He also explained the influence of the Salagou lake dug in the 1960s to collect water from the surrounding hills. I was struck by the beauty and theatricality of the place. The terroir was even more surprising. The hollow and flat schists were polyphonic, meaning they produce sounds when the wind blows. They were spread across the hillsides. '*Ruffes*', red soil that changes colour from brown to purple with the time of day reminded me of the power of telluric forces. The main house, recently built by the former owner and set on a pedestal, revealed the surrounding nature. My excitement was reaching fever pitch. I tasted a few wines from previous vintages and was impressed by their brute force and texture. I knew already how I would make them better. From the estate's launch in 2012, each day at La Sauvageonne has made me happy and connected me with the harmony of the Larzac terraces. The name of the estate reflects its wild nature, and the wines produced there, particularly from the plot next to the villa, are finely chiselled, mineral, and airy.

In 2015, the Dourthe family approached me about Château Aigues-Vives in Boutenac. I was impressed by the estate's organisation and the Bordeaux influence on the vines, tanks, and cellar. The slender and streamlined forms contrast with the more rugged topography of the Corbières. The complementarity with nearby Château Villemajou was obvious, especially with the terroir of worn pebbles, characteristic of Boutenac. Planting Syrah would create different wines, and the transition was smooth, with Jean Marie Cathary in charge.

These acquisitions and developments represent my journey to explore new horizons and create something new, driven by a commitment to terroir and a vision for the future of winemaking in Languedoc.

Clos du Temple

In 2017, my friend Jean-Claude Zabalia, a fellow traveller from the early days of my career, shared with me the problems he was facing as a partner at the Domaine de la Terre et du Temps in Cabrières. He suggested I buy the lot. Jean-Claude produced good quality red wines and continued the winegrowing tradition of this remarkable terroir, nurturing mainly old Cinsault and Grenache vines. I was overwhelmed by my first visit and understood why immediately. This is where we could elevate the reputation of rosés from the South of France to its pinnacle. Everything was there, five grape varieties: Cinsault, Grenache, Syrah, Mourvèdre, and a small plot of Viognier. The vines were old, with the sanctuary plot at the top of the dale being over eighty years old. The vines seemed to dance with each other at nightfall. The landscape was enchanting and deserved the best. This green oasis was magical. Mr Safon, the neighbour, had also put his estate up for sale. I had the idea to merge the two neighbouring estates and dedicate the parcels, which would become Clos du Temple, to the production of an exceptional rosé. This would simultaneously highlight the history of this estate built by the Templars, amortise the overall investments, and produce a top-quality red wine outside the clos. I asked Jean-Claude to stay on as a consultant to help decide the way forward. Mr Safon welcomed me one evening in his cellar. This multi-century-old building was full of history. After a two-hour discussion and a bottle of Viognier, we agreed on the terms of sale. The 2017 harvest was vinified in the old cellar. Because we picked the Grenache when it was too ripe, we decided not to put the rosé on the market. The first vintage of Clos du Temple would be 2018. Plantabelle, the red, is made from the fruit of mainly old Grenache vines grown on plots outside the Clos and overlooking the other side of the valley.

The idea to build a cellar on top of the hill came to me very quickly. I gave a tour of the estate to my Japanese friend, Katsuyuki Tanaka, and the wine critic Thierry Desseauve, and they were impressed by its power and harmony. My friend Françoise Parguel recommended François Fontès, a well-known Languedoc architect who is also a botanist and an Egyptologist. This flamboyant and uncompromising man was the right person for the job. He understood my vision, my desires, and fell under the spell of the estate. On his second visit to the vineyards and surrounding area, he gave me a precise and colourful description of the biotope. Later on, he picked up a green moss-covered pebble and told me, "Here's your cellar!" Benjamin Gadois, who was also there, and I were left speechless. After many appointments and discussions, I validated the nature of the project. This timeless and iconoclastic cellar is in harmony with the surrounding nature.

From an architectural point of view, it was conceived according to the golden ratio to help energies flow and lift matter. My idea to have pyramid-shaped tanks added a symbolic dimension, grounding the building and conveying a message of Mediterranean civilisation stretching from ancient Egypt to the present day. It is a great and proud feeling to have built a masterpiece to celebrate Cabrières wines and pay homage to our ancestors who, during the 17th century, humbly served the wine of this terroir, called 'crimson wine,' at the court of Louis XIV. This wine has been recognised year after year by the most prestigious panels of experts as one of the best and most prestigious rosés in the world.

I felt a very peculiar type of exaltation during the making of the first vintage. My desire to be true to the soul of the place moved and tormented me, and I felt deeply the weight of the responsibility to achieve the secret ambition I was nurturing. I became obsessive, making the blend time and time again with my team but also in my head. One night, I woke up suddenly. Even though everything was settled, and the final blend was ready to be bottled, I had a hunch we needed to explore a new avenue. I called Ghislain Coux, our cellarmaster, at 6 o'clock in the morning and asked him to prepare a sample of a Mourvèdre that was not currently part of the blend. By 7 o'clock, we were thinking anew, and I decided to add eleven litres of this barrel, that is 0.1%, to the blend. We put three glasses on the table, two for the initial blend and one for the new blend. We tasted them blind. There was no doubt, the addition of Mourvèdre made a significant difference and propelled the wine to a higher quality level. I was relieved and happy. I understood why I had been experiencing insomnia and a state of nervous upheaval in the previous days. I have always been guided by my intuitions, listening to the small inner voice that guides me in my permanent quest for excellence.

I have always been guided by my intuitions, listening to the small inner voice that guides me in my permanent quest for excellence.

Carcassonne Terroirs

I met Bertrand de La Soujeole in 2017. He is the heir to a long line of seventeen generations of winegrowers at the Château de La Soujeole. A bishop, he was looking for someone to continue the history of the estate. The Malepère terroir, named after the local stone used to build the city of Carcassonne, is one of the most interesting due to its topography, soils, and the freshness of its wines. The climatic influences are oceanic, and the dense vegetation is dominated by holm oaks and white oaks. Emmanuel Leroy-Ladurie, the geographer, maintained that the

Aude department was a 'little France' because of the diversity of its landscapes and climates. To understand a terroir, one must understand the surrounding biodiversity. The western and eastern hillsides are linked by a deeper terrace. The dominant grape variety is Cabernet Franc, complemented by the charm of Merlot. This still-unknown Malepère denomination offers significant taste appeal, a temperate environment, and two world-class grape varieties. Our discoverer DNA prompts us to meet the challenge. Centenarian plane trees at the entrance of the estate invite us to feel the energy of the place. Autumnal colours make the landscape look mysterious. In the west of the Languedoc, Cabernet Franc makes wines with a lot of elegance and finesse. Christophe Medinilla extracts the quintessence of this vineyard.

The terroirs of the Western Languedoc deserve particular attention. The heritage of the city of Carcassonne is cultural and historical, with its medieval theatre and its famous *cassoulet*, an ancestral recipe and popular dish that can rise to gastronomical heights. Chefs such as Jean-Claude-Rodriguez, Pierre Mesa, and André Pachon compete and promote this culinary lifestyle in France and all over the world.

In 2018, Richard Planas, our estates director, shared my analysis of the potential of these terroirs and endorsed the idea to create top-quality wines in Carcassonne. After a few trials and a biodynamic conversion, the Domaine de L'Estagnère became Castellum, a reference to the great fortified city next door. After four years of research and hard work by Guy Chiffre and his team, we identified the local potential of Sauvignon. For the red, we opted for a blend of Cabernet Sauvignon, Cabernet Franc,

Merlot, and Caladoc. After a year-long cycle of ageing, both cuvées revealed a true identity and a new freshness.

As far as Cahors

Going even further on the map of the new Occitania region, we investigated the Cahors area. This city holds many viticultural and gastronomical treasures. The meanders of the Lot River define the department's geography. This river symbolises the wealth of the region and creates magnificent landscapes. A generous nature allied with an oceanic climate allows the growth of the local black gold: the Tuber Melanos Porum truffle. The self-appointed lords of Cahors, under the aegis of remarkable personalities such as Georges Vigouroux (Château de Mercuès and Château de Haute-Serre) and Alain-Dominique Perrin (Château Lagrézette), produce distinguished, distinctive, and flavoursome wines that magnify the soul of the terroir and celebrate Malbec, the local grape variety.

Argentinians understood the nobility of this grape variety when creating its taste identity in South America. SAFER (Land Development and Rural Establishment Society) prospects on our behalf. After visiting a few estates and assessing their potential, I still hadn't fallen in love. Destiny was about to change the course of history when we took the road to Cavagnac, a hamlet in the municipality of Soturac where Serge and Martine Costes have developed a magnificent estate. We arrived at 6 p.m. in this little place where nothing ever moves. It reminded me of Burgundian villages. We got out of the car, and I immediately went for a walk in the vineyards. This siderolithic terroir packed with red iron dazzled me. It was July, and the vines looked gorgeous. Organic viticulture gives it a specific energy. The strength of the terroir and the beauty of the vines planted on gentle slopes called to me. I'd been there fifteen minutes, and I knew this is where we'd settle. The cellar and the vat-house were renovated within twelve months thanks to the know-how of our architects, Eric Martin, Nicolas, and Maxime Dornier.

The first vintage, produced in 2022, is exceptional and benefited from remarkable climatic conditions. After a gentle 12-month ageing in oak barrels, the wine spent 6 months in wooden vats before bottling. It will be released when ready to drink.

CHAPTER 2

FOUNDATIONAL ENCOUNTERS

Georges Bertrand

Georges Bertrand was the youngest of nine siblings, with his mother, Paule, born on the 1st of January 1900, serving as the cornerstone of the family. His father, Victor, who passed away too soon in 1948, hailed from Alpes-de-Haute-Provence and was a winegrower and hunter. The close bond between Georges and his mother defined his life and his love for her was deep. It wasn't easy for my mother, Geneviève, to find her place in the family initially, as we all lived together. Every evening before dinner, we spoke the local dialect when the rest of the family came over to visit Paule. Seven of my uncles were winegrowers, working alongside their wives, though their wines didn't sell well.

My father returned from the Algerian war, choosing never to speak of it, perhaps seeing no honour in fighting for a lost cause in a foreign land. He settled as a wine broker in Saint-André-de-Roquelongue, working the markets of Narbonne, Béziers, and Beaucaire. Nearing the end of his rugby career, after leading the Carnaux team to glory and playing a season for Perpignan USAP, he finished in Bizanet. The arrangement was simple: he would captain the local team and in return, become the exclusive broker for the local cooperative. From there, history was made. He would eventually taste and blend thirty thousand hectolitres of mostly red table wines and some vats of Corbières, in which he would use Grenache to soften the rough Carignan tannins. The table wine market relied then mostly on colour intensity and tannin quality.

With his first paycheck, my father bought a small vineyard and, five years later, the Domaine de Villemajou, located on the Boutenac terroir. His energy, charisma, and ambition united local winegrowers into an agricultural cooperative, creating a driving force. All the estate wines were tasted and blended by Georges, with the help and technical rigour of the Dubernet clan. This new momentum brought hope to the Languedoc. Tasting rituals were precise, held daily from 10 a.m to 12 noon and 5 p.m to 7 p.m, when samples were tallied, tasted, and sometimes analysed for their alcoholic degree. Appellation wines were classified into several categories: generic, terroir selection, estates, and châteaux. For the Villemajou estate wines, and wines of close friends like Yves Laboucarié, Jacques Bergès, and Yves Barsalou, my father's influence was evident. He insisted on picking ripe grapes, selecting plots, and vinifying rustic grape varieties using carbonic maceration to avoid astringency and bitterness. Special attention was given to centenarian vines, those that carried the memory of the place. My father's speed in tasting wines impressed me, requiring quick assessment of colour, brilliance, nose, midpalate, and length. I began taking detailed notes from my first tasting, comparing them with my father's once he had left. Differentiating between the quality and quantity of tannins was the most challenging part as the two wouldn't always balance.

I recall being invited to the blending session of the 1977 Domaine de Villemajou, the first of many. It was a great vintage. My father was excited to do his first estate bottling with his now-iconic golden label. It was January, 6 p.m., cold and dark outside, and twelve samples were lined up on the bench. We tasted them religiously, one vat after another. I still remember his words, "You'll see, sonny, we'll create a nectar." With a 100ml test tube, the standard measure for wine tasters, Georges started blending Grenache and Carignan. Then came the magical moment, "You know Gérard, the Syrah from the new vineyard we've harvested only for the second time could add something to this wine." He added 3% to the base blend, and I was dazzled by the intensified aromatic profile and complex structure. My father was pleased but not fully satisfied. "We should try with 4% and 5% to see if it makes a difference." We put down three glasses and let our sensations guide us. "The truth sits between 4 and 5%." We went for 4.5%, and as if by magic, the grape varieties aligned, tannins melded, the wine came into tension, the fieriness settled, and harmony appeared.

I was twelve and felt the desire to join this adventure, where secrets were discovered and alchemy between wines, terroirs, and people was created. My father's vision and love for Corbières drove

I was twelve and felt the desire to join this adventure, where secrets were discovered and alchemy between wines, terroirs, and people was created.

him to moderate meetings in villages, forging a path and uniting energies to elevate the area from table wines to appellation wines. This new Languedoc nobility would transcend the weight of history and petty ancestral disputes, adding value to the wines.

My father never missed an opportunity to taste bottles from different regions, often blind. "Tasting is comparing" was his favourite expression. I remember drinking the 1978 Villemajou alongside Château Mouton-Rothschild and Jaboulet's Hermitage 'La Chapelle' from the same vintages. Villemajou's harmony, in my view, already competed with Bordeaux's power and Rhône's spices. This thought fed our pride and ambition, though it was still forbidden to say it aloud. The secret remained ours, our gold standard, guiding us. My father's peculiar drive came from knowing that recognition was within reach.

Between the ages of fifteen and twenty, my tasting and blending training was shaped by my father. My studies at the Charlemagne agricultural college in Carcassonne completed my technical training, even though rugby took precedence. During the summer, my sister Guylaine and I spent every morning in the vineyards from 5 a.m. to 1 p.m., Saturdays included. Living by the rhythm of the seasons, especially between flowering and *véraison*, and then the harvest, allowed us to understand our terroir better. Winegrowing isn't a job but a leap of faith. Making one's wine is the ultimate act of faith. One must understand its meaning to elevate it, be brave

Making one's wine is the ultimate act of faith. One must understand its meaning to elevate it, be brave enough to reveal it, and embody it.

enough to reveal it, and embody it. The thousand and one details dear to Georges are the alpha and omega of my craft, combining exigency and excellence. The test of time is the best ally of a successful blend. One might think a beautiful artwork has been created, but only after ten years will it be known if the work paid off. A wine that doesn't age isn't a great wine although it can fit another category. No mistakes, arrogance, or pride are allowed. The ten-year mark is the reference for connoisseurs and applies to reds, whites, and sparkling wines, especially Champagne.

With Clos du Temple and Villa Soleilla, we've launched great rosé and orange wines, of the kind that, after ten years, will reveal secrets only great terroirs can deliver. Thanks to his intuition and pioneering work, Georges took his place in the line of winegrowers celebrated by posterity. For almost forty vintages, it's been my mission too: keeping the torch aflame, cautiously climbing the ladder, and opening a new chapter and era for the wines of my region.

Since my father's accidental death on the 28th of October 1987, I've had many conversations with him in my head. His presence has been everywhere, guiding my acts and my thoughts, his soul shining bright in the universe where I liked to seek refuge to connect with his spiritual energy. I could hear him say, "Gérard, have faith, don't be sad, life will teach you important lessons. Continue and carry the flame further. Take care of everybody and, moreover, enjoy every single minute." His vital force, creative spirit, and generous smile are indelible, a permanent testimony, a chapter in the big book of life.

This continuum of know-how fits into a story that started two thousand four hundred years ago with ancient Greece, which brought us the first grape varieties, then the Romans who settled Narbonne, Narbo Martius, and organised our region. Since then, the Mediterranean has traded wines and celebrated the worship of Dionysus. Georges understood this: he was a knight, and his quest was inspired by a mystical momentum.

Dubernet, fathers and sons

Jean-Henri, Marc, Mathieu: three generations, almost a dynasty, who watch over the world's largest wine region, Occitania, with energy, expertise, and know-how even though other players, notably the Institut Coopératif du Vin, the preferred technical partner of cooperative cellars for a long time, have also significantly contributed to the region's wine quality through the efforts of talented individuals.

The Dubernet family exemplifies unique kinship, family values, and ambition. Jean-Henri, the pioneer and experimenter, was among the first to bridge empirical practices with the emerging science of oenology. Marc, the researcher, and master of engineering and applied sciences, is also a tireless taster, adapting to the evolving viticulture landscape. Inspired by his forebearers, Mathieu recognises the importance of going beyond oenology to enhance soil capabilities for balanced, climate-resilient vines while meeting market demands.

Their journey reflects three economic stages: the gathering economy, where production relied on natural offerings; the production economy, regulating global consumption and ensuring prosperity in regions like Champagne, Bordeaux, and Burgundy; and the market economy, realistic, unforgiving, and globalised, that allowed the rise of the New World - notably Australia, Chile and Argentina - and changed the perception of consumers' tastes.

In the 1960s and 1970s, winegrowing wasn't seen as an economic activity but as a way to quench the thirst of the French, who each consumed 120L of wine per annum. Quality was a nascent concept, with fine wines representing only 1% of total production. Transitioning to estate bottling and developing the appellation concept required courage. It was a different era. Land pressure was non-existent, and business was managed prudently and responsibly. There was no point in planning ahead as most trade was in bulk, with wine shipped in barrels from quays in Bordeaux, Marseille, Sete, or trading posts in Algiers and Tunis. Wine was more of a beverage than the sublime nectar it is today.

Jean-Henri Dubernet

Jean-Henri anticipated change, sharing the best oenological and hygiene practices to ensure clean and continuous fermentation. His approach included precise gestures, adherence to processes, the use of selected yeasts, grape sorting, and appropriate cellar equipment, all ingredients of a new paradigm, reviving the Languedoc. Jean-Henri was part of a small group determined to save the region from its anticipated decline.

He focused on developing a taste identity and updating specifications with listed grape varieties, yield limits, and aging lengths in all the villages of the Corbières, Minervois and elsewhere in the Mediterranean area. Jean-Henri tirelessly traversed the region, day after day and seven days a week during the harvest, offering with remarkable composure and wisdom, practical and essential advice to those eager to produce good wines. Though the time for operational excellence hadn't yet arrived, some initiatives produced quality cuvées, instilling pride in winegrowers and achieving critical success for the best wines.

The desire to be recognised by others and earn expert approval was crucial for those with aspirations for better winemaking. The era of pioneers is often marked by solidarity or mutual encouragement, fostering the drive to continue.

I remember meeting Jean-Henri during my first years as a winemaker and tasting with him under my father's protective gaze. I was still a child and listened to their conversations which, from vat to vat and according to the progress of fermentations, would guide the winemaking process and assess the future potential of the wine. I was in awe of the elegance and the poise of this tall and slender gentleman, with his scarf around his neck. He used to write down priorities in a little notebook and promised to return within forty-eight hours. His camaraderie with Georges was evident and his visits, three or four times a week, would fulfil Georges' need for information and calm his anxieties. In an era where common sense and experience were primary guides, the family oenologist held a role akin to that of a GP or a priest. He attended family events and sometimes influenced winery investments.

Men who started from scratch built their reputations slowly at a time when barriers were hard to break down. Jackie Kennedy serving Petrus at the White House marked the beginning of a legend. Alexis Lichine, whose son Sacha helped to lift the profile of Provence rosés, travelled the United States to promote his wines and his brands at a time when export sales were limited although people drank well, mostly champagne or Bordeaux in embassies and diplomacy circles, especially in the West. This pioneer era was fascinating, be it in New York, London or Tokyo. Wine was bizarrely the providential drink that would lift the most prestigious dinners but also the drink of choice for workers in factories, fields or vineyards.

Marc Dubernet

Marc initially had to gain acceptance from the family hierarchy. He didn't escape this type of education where every progress has to be deserved. After the era of the pioneer came that of the conqueror. Jean-Henri faded away and Marc took over the business. With intelligence, spirit, and ambition, he contributed to speeding up and accompanying the quality revolution that was underway. His approach was obviously more scientific and structured than Jean-Henri's. Physicochemical analysis was becoming finer and more precise, shedding light on the viticultural journey. Marc has the confidence of those who know the answers to the most complex questions and can anticipate problems. He probably attracted professional jealousies as being ahead of one's time is never easy. Having never had the opportunity to enter politics, he stayed focused on the essential. Data computerisation, automation of blending calculations and microbiological research held no secret for him.

From November 1987 to now, we have shared four decades of work, passionate exchanges and remarkable blends. His encyclopaedic knowledge, open-mindedness, and interest in new technologies have supported the rise of the Languedoc. Michel Rolland had a different impact as the size, organisation and issues of Bordeaux and the Languedoc cannot be compared. Michel was a tireless advocate of French expertise and won over the New World by sharing the techniques and know-how that would lead to success. Marc chose another, more orthodox, route, that of the oenologist at the service of all types of viticulture. The resurgent Languedoc needed more methods and processes to guarantee the essential: the quality of taste. The trend towards premium quality was already ongoing but at a slower pace. Marc has the ascetic discipline and strength to taste for seven to eight hours a day over four months and to lift each estate upwards. His experience and ability to decipher an estate are impressive. He can immediately recognise the elements essential to the future blend and identify the troublemakers.

I didn't train as an oenologist and have always had a more empirical and sensitive approach to blending than him, but our conclusions were often in line. The rare occasions when we disagreed were usually a bad sign for the vintage. Obviously, the Domaine de Villemajou represents the alpha of our relationship.

Olfactive memory is as impressive as visual memory: sharing forty vintages in a lifespan and having the opportunity to double up with Jean-Claude Berrouet over twenty years has been my open university experience. Both of these men have been my personal doctor *honoris causa.*

The spread of my purchases, year after year, has helped develop a close relationship with Marc. The Cigalus, Laville-Bertrou, La Sauvageonne and l'Hospitalet estates, among the better known, have shown their best with his help and that of my teams, including Richard Planas, the cornerstone of my estate management team, as well as Ghislain Coux, my faithful and talented general cellarmaster.

After taking over Château l'Hospitalet in 2002, an overhaul of the technical processes was needed to give soul to the wine: reviewing balances, enhancing terroir typicity and fruit expression more than oak expression, and selecting the best plots. When one decides to start from a blank page, excitement is at its peak. The emotion at the end of the first session was unreal. I remember bursting with happiness and singing in the car on my way back to the office as if I'd won a rugby final. More recently when I bought Château La Sauvageonne in 2012, situated in the magnificent terroir of the Larzac terraces, I was fascinated, struck afresh by so much beauty. This unique schist and volcanic soil terroir deeply inspires me and soothes my senses. The first vintages - 2012, 2013, 2014 – were very good but unpopular. They lacked strength of character. Languedoc Syrah has such aromatic potential that it can sometimes, in some difficult terrains, take over and completely dominate a blend.

After witnessing the birth of the 2015 vintage, I conceived an idea over several weeks. I arrived at 8 a.m. at the blending session. We were all there. Mathieu Dubernet had joined the team a few seasons previously and was beginning to assert his opinion. Marc and I had grown so close that we were able to understand each other without talking. I set out facts, maybe a touch solemnly. "Dear friends, we have now crafted three vintages, the necessary time to understand a terroir, grape varieties and the soul of a place. To be honest with you, I am not entirely satisfied with the result of our work. I've had an idea though: let's create the blend around Grenache and reduce the percentage of Syrah, without changing anything to the additional grape varieties, that do not exceed 15% of the blend when combined."

We started the blending session. 2015 is a great vintage but a touch sunny. The summer was hot and dry. Grenache can withstand such high temperatures, but Syrah likes cooler soils. Volcanic soils, called *ruffes*, need water towards the end of the summer. The mid-September rain was a blessing to unblock this cycle of berry maturation and enhance the mineral imprint of the wine. After tasting all the plots, we talked and picked up the selected plots for the top cuvée. Under my guidance, we tried a blend with over 60% Grenache. It showed no balance, the wine was flat and out of tune. We spent the morning working and trying different formulas. Nothing worked. It was chaos!

It is very rare to stop a session after almost five hours spent looking for a solution. The more time passed, the further away from what we were looking for we got. Marc, wisely, recommended we call it a day and suggested a date two weeks later. It is essential to have the humility to give time to a project, as time only can give thinking space and altruism. Like good wine, it is often necessary to let ideas decant to take them further. The door may open more easily on another day. It is what happened, and the second session gave birth in less than two hours to the new spirit of Château La Sauvageonne: a distinguished, typical, taut, mineral wine with controlled generosity, intense fruit and a silky length.

Only communion of minds can reveal the quintessence of a unique place. When you are on the right track and that alchemy

Our knowing smiles lit up the room. This shared intensity of pain initially and then of joy is characteristic of our craft. We are not winegrowers or oenologists, we become alchemists and look for the philosophical stone, the key that will open the door to the temple and reveal all its secrets.

between grape varieties and plots aligns, you enter a new dimension, one where wine tells a story, consistent with the surrounding ecosystem and the tradition outlined by the work of the winegrowers. Our knowing smiles lit up the room. This shared intensity of pain initially and then of joy is characteristic of our craft. We are not winegrowers or oenologists, we become alchemists and look for the philosophical stone, the key that will open the door to the temple and reveal all its secrets.

Mathieu Dubernet

Mathieu stayed in his father's footsteps for a long time, starting young while Marc was at the pinnacle of his career. He took time to grow, observe, and identify his next steps to progress further. This family link, this desire to support winegrowers, and this unwavering humility are the Dubernet trademarks. The challenges of 21st-century winegrowing and the demands of trade globalisation compel all stakeholders in the wine world to redefine their priorities and strengthen perceived quality. The Anglo-Saxon system, built around grape varieties, shakes up the certainties of the Old World, organised in small structures and around terroirs as in France, Italy, Spain, Portugal, and Greece.

Mathieu travels and exports his family know-how, first to the Rhône Valley, then Provence and abroad. His transverse approach between soils and wines opens possibilities and helps to understand how grape varieties function. Understanding the absorption of trace elements and their ability to stimulate the plant and improve the quality of wines propels oenology into a new era. From now on, the initial empirical approach, supplemented with basic oenology and accompanied by ancestral know-how, will need to draw from the latest discoveries to progress and ceaselessly meet the ever-growing demands from consumers and wine lovers. Mathieu understands the need to go from know-how to making it known. He is one of the opinion leaders of the wine industry, in charge of a transformation while considering not just the long-time scale of appellations but also the challenges of international competition and the high stakes of quality, competitiveness, climates, and trends. He draws upon the exceptional tasting and blending expertise of his father and knows how to find his own style to take it further. His talents and drive carry on the family tradition and align with the necessities of precision winemaking.

Jean-Claude Berrouet

In the spring of 1989, I was invited to a symposium about barrel ageing at the abbey of Notre-Dame-de-Gaussan, in Bizanet, in the Corbières. Aged twenty-four, I was eager to learn and understand the mechanics of wine, from winemaking to bottling. Ageing is split into two parts: the time spent in oak vats or barrels and the longer time devoted to bottle ageing. The length of barrel ageing varies between one and three years for some appellations, especially in Spain where wines can be classified either Reserva or Gran Reserva. In France and in countries where the influence of French oenologists dominates, ageing is often characterised by the rhythm of the four seasons, that is more or less twelve months. Sometimes, depending on the vintage, the process of tannin polymerisation and managed oxidation has to be extended by a few weeks.

In 1973, my father was a pioneer: he bought second-hand barrels from Château Dassault in Saint-Emilion and was one of the first winegrowers to age Languedoc wines in oak barrels. This experience was a significant step towards better quality and ageing potential at the Domaine de Villemajou. The expression of a wine, its identity, develops during this time spent in the cellar's shadows and under controlled temperature and humidity conditions. Jean-Claude Berrouet, the master of ceremonies, appeared in front of an audience of two hundred people, mostly neighbouring winegrowers. He faced his public, sitting on a slightly raised desk, his only prop an oak stave. A long and methodical ninety-minute monologue started. I was struck by the accuracy of his words, the tone of his voice, the precision of the details he gave, and moreover by the closeness he easily created with his audience using clear and easy-to-understand language. This man from the South-West of France spoke with the singing accent of the Basque country and the conviction and wisdom of someone who knows and masters the art of rhetoric. I took notes and savoured this story that managed to be at the same time historical and technical. Only the time already spent honing his craft allowed him to fathom these essential observations for the teaching of vine and wine. His unparalleled expertise of Bordeaux since the 1960s, his willingness to travel and discover the New World, opened new vistas and generated clear opinions.

Jean-Claude likes classicism. A classical wine tells the story of its terroir, adaptation to grape varieties and climate, and transcends the experience. Jean-Claude beams; his charisma and aura resonate with those who understand that men are at the service of terroir, seeking the soul of a place, the soil character, without stylistic effects. Style is fashion, fleeting and ephemeral, linked to a trend. Jean-Claude understood, with his characteristic humility, that with classified Grands Crus, man should take a step back and simply accompany history. Much later, when coming back to this moment, I took the liberty to remind him that it is much easier to take a step back when your ancestors have already forged the route ahead and charted a story.

At the end of the masterclass, the director of the Camplong cellar asked him an odd question: "Mr Berrouet, we have in the cellar a very good 1985 wine. Is it possible to age it in barrels ?" With a hint of humour and the agility of a torero in the Bayonne arenas, Jean-Claude pushed back gently, and reminded him of the essential: "The wine has already been aged in vats for three years, the last thing it needs is more oxidation. Dear Sir, bottle it as soon as possible".

After this brilliant speech, I rushed over to greet him: 'Good morning, Sir, my name is Gérard Bertrand, Corbières winegrower.' He stopped me, "I know you! You play rugby for Narbonne and I knew your father very well. Jean-Henri Dubernet, my internship supervisor in the 1960s, introduced me to him." We chatted for ten minutes, and he suggested I visit him at home whenever convenient.

January 1990. I arrived in Libourne at 8 a.m. I had in my suitcase the 1989 Domaine de Villemajou, to taste with this remarkable man. The Holy Grail for a beginner! Jean-Claude welcomed me with great kindness and simplicity. We lined up the thirty bottles of the new vintage. The estate had grown since the 1970s and we now produced a little over two thousand hectolitres on sixty hectares. Jean-Claude carefully opened the bottles one after the other, put the corks down, meticulously replaced the bottles back in the lineup, and handed over a glass to me. The name of the plot, the grape variety, and the number of hectolitres were written on each label. The aim was to make the best possible wine. I worked towards the production of a minimum number of bottles in order to fulfil our clients' orders, and if possible, to conquer new markets. If I were to translate this into a mathematical equation, we would have four variables and therefore billions of possibilities: thirty-five plots, thirty-five different volumes, four grape varieties, and a minimum number of bottles to produce. Place your bets, no more bets!

There are two ways to proceed: either a wholly empirical approach when you taste the wines and let destiny and intuition do the rest, or a more rational approach when you identify the best plots and remember the history of years gone by as well as which grape variety proportions created the best balances. Jean-Claude Berrouet's approach is a sophisticated blend of intelligence, feeling, experience, and analysis. He is like a tennis player who masters all the shots and can play on every surface. We both jotted down our tasting notes for each lot, taking care first to benchmark the different grape varieties, as he was interested in my lived experience.

At the end of the first session, Jean-Claude made a few general comments on the vintage potential. It was a great-quality year and the balance between tannins, acidity and sugars was already good. We tasted the 1988 vintage - my first vintage, still in barrel - for Jean-Claude to absorb a bit more of the DNA of the estate. He suggested we both work on our own blend, and we got started. I couldn't help watching him work. He kneeled down in order to be at the height of the bottle, and to pour the wine in the test tube with the precision of a Swiss clockmaker. He told me that this physically demanding exercise is essential to ensure that the visual analysis of the wine is aligned with the selected volume.

For the first lesson, we each tasted the other's blend. Jean-Claude had created a 1,300-hectolitre blend and me an 850-hectolitre blend. His was more elegant than mine but lacked a bit in structure. Mine was more powerful but lacked enough finesse. Jean-Claude explained it is always easier to decrease than to increase and that we should never miss the opportunity to blend the largest possible volume, if quality justifies it.

For the second lesson, we combined our thoughts and intuitive efforts. Jean-Claude explained that no one can get the quintessence of a blending session on their own. Only teamwork leads to finding the perfect balance. It can be achieved in one session but seldom, and it is usually necessary, especially when the initial volume and the number of samples are high, to work in stages, as our mouth and palate reach their tasting capacity after three to four hours of intense tasting. Saliva dries up and doesn't allow for proper hydration of the mouth sensors. By the end of the morning, we had created three blends of different volumes, and we tasted them. Jean-Claude covered each glass with a sheet of paper to keep the fruit and avoid excessive oxidation during our lunch break. We went to the Chanzy, a restaurant located in the eponymous street, close to Libourne station. Jean-Claude had his habits there. The owner, who doubled up as a waiter, listed the dishes of the day. South-West gastronomy, and Bordeaux's in particular, is always tempting. Very often, Bordeaux-style lamprey, a classic dish, is recommended. Jean-Claude ordered a bottle of his estate's wine, Vieux Château-Saint-André, from Montagne-Saint-Emilion, and a bottle of Château Bélair, Saint-Émilion grand cru. We talked freely about wine, rugby, and mutual friends. These two wines from the 1980s were tasting very well. Jean-Claude is without equal when it comes to revealing terroir and finding balance. I am always impressed by the poetry and the magic that infuse his scientific culture, like Yin and Yang, the two sides of the same coin. A wine construction, for Jean-Claude, isn't just an academic exercise. His classical culture, shaped by Émile Peynaud, has been magnified by his genius and his unique sensibility.

Jean-Claude is without equal when it comes to revealing terroir and finding balance. I am always impressed by the poetry and the magic that infuse his scientific culture, like Yin and Yang, the two sides of the same coin.

To resonate with a vintage, place and grape varieties while reaching out to the owner to absorb the background, history and tradition of an estate in order to find the true path, a path that may never have been dared or taken, requires asceticism, a profession of faith and an open mind.

To create the conditions of success, everything matters. Light is very important – the light of day but also that of bulbs that must be as close as possible to natural light. The bench will be white to show the wine's brightness. The panelling will be light and unwaxed, not to interfere with olfactory sensors. Utensils, test tubes, and measuring cylinders, will be made of glass and clearly marked to avoid any mistakes. Everybody has their favourite tasting glass. Force of habit drives us to keep the same glass throughout the tasting and always for blending exercises.

This doesn't apply to lunches or dinners where legendary glassmakers such as Riedel, Lehman or Zalto vie with creativity and sensitivity to supply the glassware. Oddly enough, ordinary glasses with which we have established reliable sensory benchmarks are used for blending.

As the years went by, from 1990 to 2010, my Libourne trip

became a tradition. We have tasted twenty-one vintages of Villemajou together. This timeless day has always kept a friendly, almost brotherly tone. Jean-Claude shaped my learning and my vision of the profession. He may have detected my willpower and thirst for knowledge. Our sensitivities were definitely compatible and in tune.

After this long sequence, I've had the opportunity to taste with him and Jean-François, his son, in my sanctuary at Château l'Hospitalet. Only after he retired did he agree to become an official advisor to blending Clos d'Ora. Jacques Dupont, the reference for wines at *Le Point* magazine in the early 2000s – in the middle of Parkermania – had the foresight and wisdom to write an article dedicated to Jean-Claude Berrouet, entitled '*The Last of the Just*'. In it, he praised the respect of terroir as opposed to excessive oak ageing that disguises wines and hides their identity. Resisting the opinion of well-known critics and fashions is brave and courageous.

Jean-Claude always claimed that a great wine wasn't made to be tasted but to be drunk. The moment of truth at the end of a meal is whether bottles are empty. All wines, and especially the greatest ones, should be thirst-quenching.

Marcel Rouillé

To be Catalan in the world of wine, as in the world of literature, means demanding, or even fighting for, this identity that Salvador Dalí knew how to glorify. This culture is shared between the Pyrénées-Orientales department in the north and southern Catalonia. The administrative frontier at Perthus is the link between the two territories. The crimson and golden colours are signs of recognition and belonging to this lifestyle. Perpignan and her big sister, Barcelona, embody this pride but also this wealth. The town of Girona, located between the two, affirms this Catalan pride to the point of breaking with conventions in an affirmed desire for autonomy. Marcel belongs to the majority of this people, who through wisdom and flair, has a moderate and altruistic vision of the future of the area.

Between the summit of the Canigou, the Carlit peak at 1,980 metres altitude, and the Mediterranean Sea, French Catalonia, also called Roussillon, is home to riches and a unique artisanal and winemaking know-how. In the 13th century, the chemist Arnaud de Villeneuve invented mutage, a fortification method where grape juice fermentation is stopped by the addition of alcohol. This innovative process allowed the creation of a new category of wines, later called *vins doux naturel*s (VDN). These now iconic wines brought wealth to the area. They use mostly the Muscat à petits grains and Muscat of Alexandria grape varieties to make Muscat de Rivesaltes. There are three different denomination areas for red wines. Rivesaltes is amber or *tuilé*, that is dark ruby with lighter edges, and its colour depends on the proportion of grape varieties in the blend: Grenache Noir, Grenache Gris and Macabeu. Maury is mostly made from Grenache Noir. The Banyuls appellation makes red wines with both Grenache grape varieties, but also white wines and some Grands Crus. This terroir, stretching from Collioure to Port-Vendres, is very steep. It is a natural masterpiece, nature tamed by man, with vines grown on terraces that are very picturesque and demanding.

Marcel Rouillé, after studying oenology and playing professional rugby, was part of the quality and identity step up of Roussillon wines. He was the driving force of ICV, the Institut Coopératif du Vin, and contributed to the advent of the cooperative sector. Later on, he also contributed to the creation of some iconic wines when advising private cellars. Although competing with Jean Rière and more recently with Jean Michel Barcelo, my college friend, he supported them in strengthening the identity of Roussillon crus.

This department took a definite advantage from its proximity to Spain, but also confirmed its strategic positioning with the Saint-Charles de Perpignan market. This market acts as a European platform for fruit and vegetables and a logistical bridgehead between Spain and the rest of Europe, to the detriment of local produce that declined because of a lack of competitiveness.

The production of dry wines and *vins doux naturels* held up until 2000 before volumes decreased because of land pressure due to rising tourism in the area. The dry and hot climate of the region and the soil geology caused the cost of winegrowing, and therefore of wines, to rise.

Marcel Rouillé always had a clear vision of Roussillon

winegrowing and advocated a subtle blend between dry wines and *vins doux naturels*. The time of *mistelles** and vermouths, formerly flagbearers for the area, is behind us. The Byrrh brand notably, brought wealth to local villages and built cathedral-like cellars in Thuir or Tautavel, to age these wines.

The challenge of the last twenty years was to switch to the production of dry wines, fresher and easier to drink, while managing the predicted decline of *vins doux naturels*. This project succeeded and brought with it both a generational and winegrowing and winemaking change. Marcel's genius helped create these wines, better suited to the taste of consumers. He, however, didn't neglect the cuvées of *vins doux naturels*, thinking fifty years ahead to perpetuate the myth of these legendary wines.

The novel approach of this talented winemaker entailed introducing new winemaking techniques, very different for dry wines and *vins doux naturels*, developing grape selection according to terroir and picking grapes at optimal maturity. Grenache needs to be picked very ripe for *vins doux naturels* and earlier for dry wines to preserve the fresh fruit aromas and avoid the oxidation that is desirable in *vins doux naturels*. Making long-term choices also means the winegrower must free himself from market trends.

The paradox in this French department has always been to try and balance the small yields per hectare with market demands and consumers' needs. "You can never have too much of a good thing", is a Latin saying that is particularly accurate here but requires choices.

---

*Mistelles are products produced from unfermented fresh grapes or grape musts (1% vol. actual alcohol is tolerated) and rendered non-fermentable by addition of wine spirit.

Marcel was a precious ally in implementing a partnership with winegrowers from the Tautavel Cru. With his help and that of Régis Ouguères, Caves de Tautavel chairman, we brought together four cooperative cellars, fostered their rapprochement to create different cuvées and sell more than 80% of the Cru wines throughout the world. Understanding the identity of this incredible place and forging a link between the winegrowers of Tautavel, Vingrau, and Estagel required patience, interpersonal skills, and love for a cause that goes beyond the world of wine.

Tautavel is home to the history of humankind, as demonstrated by its anthropology museum. French archaeologist, geologist and prehistorian, Henri de Lumley, and his wife, discovered the bones of the oldest prehistoric man, dated from 140,000 years BC, and continue their research with the help of an amazing operational team of scientists from over fifty different countries worldwide. Their visceral need to bear witness to the evolution of mankind covers all eras from Australopithecus, Neanderthals, and different variants of Homo sapiens. The Tautavel museum is a multigenerational heirloom that gives sense to the thousand-year-old winegrowing tradition and gives it meaning. The area's wines have identity and expression. They are like no others and carry within them a unique and authentic character. With Marcel Rouillé and the precision of Stéphane Queralt, also Roussillon born, we have built, year after year, the outlines of different vintages. We continue today this collective task and spread the good word Urbi et Orbi*.

* Urbi et Orbi, literally means 'to the city (of Rome) and to the world' and refers to the papal blessing that is extended to the whole world on different occasions.

Tasting history

The most beautiful adventure with Marcel Rouillé began the day he left the ICV – Institut Coopératif du Vin. I called him and suggested he help me curate a collection of old *vins doux naturels* and introduce me to this world of well-kept secrets, mostly guarded by the great Roussillon families. Tradition is preserved from generation to generation, and the family heirloom means much more than a father-to-son or daughter transition. It is a patrimony, a history, and a know-how that get passed on and recounted time and time again.

Mrs. Villa, over eighty years old, welcomed me to the village of Saint-Estève. She had the conviction and character of those who had lived through the difficulties of the Second World War, the rise of mixed farming, and the desire to create timeless wines. I tasted a few Côtes-du-Roussillon with her before embarking on a vertical tasting of Rivesaltes: 1982, 1978, 1974, and a sublime 1959. The first ones were aged in wooden vats, and the 1959 in concrete vats. We were in 2000, meaning over forty years of slow ageing. This wine, made exclusively from Grenache Noir, was amazing and tasted incredibly young. Its ageing had preserved its black fruit aromas and slowed down its oxidation.

Mrs. Villa shared the story of her wines, revealing that her late husband had told her that 1959 was an exceptional vintage. This life story was touching and celebrated the unique character of these memory wines. It created a mysterious intimacy and a special language. Time contracted, bringing us back to what is essential – giving meaning to life – and creating the kind of different time spaces that generate amazement and ecstasy. We bottled this 1959 treasure, which became the first but not the oldest vintage of this budding collection.

The Terrats winegrowers had several vintages ageing in their cellars. I was enchanted by the 1974, a blend of Grenache Noir, Grenache Gris, and Macabeu. Aged in barrels, wooden vats, and concrete vats, it had developed unparalleled aromas of dried fruit, vanilla, and a peated aftertaste, reminiscent of bourbons enjoyed while smoking a cigar. Its reasonable price allowed us to buy 30,000 bottles.

We also developed a few vintages of Banyuls from the Côte Vermeille. These wines from terroirs next to the sea are a gift to Mediterranean civilisation, with delicacy, charm, and amazing complexity, best enjoyed with a lemon tart or a bowl of strawberries.

Further north, the Maury winegrowers keep a unique tradition, terroir, and know-how. Within a day, from 9 a.m. to 6 p.m., I had the privilege to taste over forty vintages going back to 1950. Tasting these wines transports you and arouses strong feelings. The intensity of aromas, colour nuances, and the multidimensional finish put you in an alternative state of mind connecting terroir with the core of your being. These are authentic wines offering unique sensations, incredibly difficult to resist swallowing.

The intensity of aromas, colour nuances, and the multidimensional finish put you in an alternative state of mind connecting terroir with the core of your being.

Not giving in is torture. Each nectar plays a melodious yet different harmony. You must know when to stop, take a break, and return to a regular tasting rhythm to understand the score of each vintage better. We liked the 1977, 1955, and 1951 best. I recommend they be enjoyed with dark chocolate and dried fruit puddings.

My meeting with Georges Puig, a colourful character, started at 10 a.m. in the village of Passa. We tasted Rivesaltes from 1945 to 1990, offering a range of pleasures and emotions. Georges, the custodian of a family heritage going back to the 19th century, takes his time. When you carry a hundred and fifty years of history, you do not rush. He invited Marcel and me to stay for lunch and brought up a few bottles of wine and *vins doux naturels* from the cellar. His family house defies classification, full of secrets, joys, and tragedies. Browsing the harvest photo albums, the energy and mettle of his ancestors leap off the page. Both his grandfathers were part of the Rugby League and Rugby Union French team. The most surprising and moving fact of these family memories is the passion of these two men, who humbly and mindfully came home to harvest every year. They were the keepers of a project much bigger than them that offers them a role in Dionysus' story.

At five o'clock, we entered a small cellar where an assortment of old barrels, *feuillantines* (small sixty-litre barrels), and glass jars were stored. Surprises were just beginning. We started with an incredibly deeply coloured and powerful 1918. This wine celebrated the end of the First World War and the beginning of a new era for our country. France recovered from this tragedy albeit slowly. This vintage spoke of new impetus and strengthened energy. We continued with the 1914, the opposite of the previous wine, marked by the intense suffering of the people.

Next was 1910, a year marked by big floods in Paris and the death of Tolstoy in Russia, but also the will of the people to free themselves from the constraints of the 19th century. The wine was black and very concentrated. In those days, winegrowers would blend according to what was planted in the vineyard. It was common to find different grape varieties in one plot, including Carignan for structure, the perfect blending partner of Grenache.

The year 1900 celebrated the end of the post-industrial world and the beginning of the century of huge changes. Born that year, my grandmother, Paule Bertrand, had in her the desire for empowerment, a dream of a better world and the energy to fight and earn a more ambitious future for women. Entering a new century is a rare and symbolical time, manifested then by the Universal Exhibition in Paris. 1900 was a legendary vintage in the southern half of France. In Bordeaux and Sauternes, wines were delicious. The *vin doux naturel* is remarkably fresh. It offers a very complex aromatic palette, blending black fruit, dried fruit, blond tobacco, sweet spices, a full mouth and a remarkable vibration.

We moved on to the 19th century, preserved in *feuillantines*. We continued with 1895, a year of wars multiplying in Asia and Africa. Lenin rallied Marxists in Russia to free the working class before being arrested and imprisoned for three years. Harvests in 1895 were very good in Champagne, Bordeaux, and Roussillon. The wine had an amber colour with bright highlights and aromas of dry rancio. The aromatic complexity was unusual, blending hazelnut, walnut, raisins, and cinnamon. The palate was intense and characterised by a controlled evolution. The finish went on forever and opened the door to Bacchus's heaven. This wine would be a great match for an old Comté or Cantal.

1890 was a transitional year, marking the end of the Great Depression and the beginning of the second industrial revolution, notable for innovations in the field of petrol, cars, textiles, and chemistry. The 1890 vintage was marked by a cold spring and a month of September with dry and hot days and cool nights, ideal for the creation of long-lived wines. The wine was amber in colour with yellow-orange highlights. Aromas were subtle and complex. Swirling the wine in the glass repeatedly revealed an evolution delivering unending pleasure and sensations, from dried fruit – almonds, hazelnuts, cashew nuts – to stone fruit and roasted chocolate aromas. The palate was harmonious and elegant, balancing the bitterness of dark chocolate and sweet spices, supported by a tight and taut structure. The finish made you want more, with the freshness of the wine coming as a pleasant surprise.

1875 marked the advent of the third Republic in France and the return of the monarchy in Spain. In Germany, Bismarck threatened France with war and entered into open conflict with the clergy. The United Kingdom strengthened its hold on waterways through the purchase of a majority of the shares of the Suez Canal. 1875 is remembered as the greatest vintage of the 19th century with highly balanced, elegant, and refined wines. The 1875 *vin doux naturel* didn't let this legendary vintage down: the colour was dark and evolved. Aromas were powerful and intoxicating, expressing a subtle blend of honey, cinnamon, currant, and fruit preserved in alcohol. The mouth was taut and vinous. The powerful structure initially masked the sweetness. The aftertaste took us further with salted caramel, vanilla, hints of dark chocolate, and a beautiful bitterness. It finished on an array of sensations, an invitation to meditation and transcendence.

It was late. When we left the cellar, night had already fallen. We had been there only for a few hours, but it felt like time had stood still. We had not only tasted these man-made treasures, but we had also drunk them. We were joyful and intoxicated by these grace-filled and weightless moments. Georges suggested we stay for dinner. We could only accept to extend this memorable day, continuing our conversation while drinking all the wines we had tasted with typical Catalan dishes: anchovies, of course, but also *boles de picolat*, these famous meatballs made of pork and beef. We were facing two centuries of history of this magnificent area. I was deeply moved, thanked my friend Marcel, and thanked life for treating me to this unbelievable day. We chatted, putting the world to rights until midnight, and finished all the little bottles collected from the cellars. We also agreed on the next steps. My deepest desire was to include five of the oldest vintages in the Legend Vintage range. I told Georges I wouldn't try to negotiate the price and went home with my memories of this unique day and the certainty that my job is the best in the world. We completed our portfolio of *vins doux naturels* with twenty bottles of each of the five oldest vintages.

Marcel and I travelled the length and breadth of the Pyrénées-Orientales department, meeting amazing winegrowers, men and women, proud of their heritage and aware of their role as connectors between generations. We managed to collect more than forty vintages spanning one hundred and fifty years. These wines are now part of my family's heritage and will be released in small batches each year, sharing the soul of this region over several decades.

Katsuyuki Tanaka

Tokyo, May 2012. Japan is celebrating cherry blossoms. The capital city is waking up from the wintery cold and young people are raring to be free. I am always impressed by the traditions and rituals of the Japanese people, the well-established framework of social and professional relationships. This ancestral and pyramidal organisation guarantees a form of stability but is also cumbersome for free-minded spirits. The debate about school uniforms evokes the discipline and respect felt by all the boys and girls met in the streets of Tokyo and all over Japan. Their nationalistic pride is strong, and their dedication to their country is palpable.

It took me a few years to understand how to establish commercial relationships with my distributors. The "yes" that characterises an agreement in the West doesn't mean the same in Japan. "Yes" means "I understand." Culturally, it is difficult, nay impossible, for a Japanese person to say no during a meeting, as it would go against the rules of courtesy. Friendship codes are highly scripted and hierarchical, and going from the status of client to that of loyal friend and then close friend takes a lot of time, not an easy thing for a young Frenchman in a hurry as I was in the 1990s. It's only through studying history and showing a lot of respect and patience that it is possible to slowly decipher the behaviour of our commercial contacts and understand their character.

It is 1.30 pm, and I am reaching the end of a lunch- cum-tasting in a very good restaurant. My guests, mostly journalists, are sharing a unique food and wine matching experiment. Japanese cuisine, rich in culinary treasures, offers rare matches, especially with the umami flavour. This sapid intensity from dried and grated bonito is a match for savoury, sweet, acidic and bitter flavours. It undulates between sweetness and iodine, with a soft and concentrated texture.

In terms of wines, the Japanese market is classical and upmarket. Wine consumption is quite small and often limited to special occasions, particularly towards the end of the year. You wouldn't drink a glass of wine to go with lunch during the week, even if the opening of a few wine bars is starting a new trend, especially among young people.

My first distributor taught me the virtue of patience. I understood that we were really in business when the managing director invited me to the office of the chairman, on the top floor. The sense of protocol is very elaborate in the Land of the Rising Sun. Drinking tea and spending half an hour with the owner of the company signalled a new alliance.

Our distributor's loyalty is absolute, as is his respect for commercial confidentiality. In Japan, commitments are honoured but flexibility isn't a forte. You could call relationships conservative. It took me a long time to understand why Japanese people didn't drink rosé when this wine is a natural match for sushi and sashimi. After attempting several times to convince prominent personalities such as Yumi Tanabe, one of the most influential women in wine in Asia, I had to admit the obvious conclusion. These dishes are consumed with green tea and sake, and the protection of local traditions is immutable.

Under the patronage of Yumi, who created the Sakura Women's Wine Awards, a competition celebrating the best wines in the world, women are however having an increasing impact in this market. 2019 Hospitalitas was acknowledged as the best red wine worldwide by this panel of women judges.

A few years earlier, we received an order for five thousand bottles of La Forge, half of the volume produced. Olivier, our production director, called me as he didn't understand what was happening. I didn't either, and nor did Jan Wisser, our Asia commercial director. After some research, we discovered that this wine was featured in an episode of one of the most popular manga series about wine in Japan. I travelled over there for public relations purposes and was stopped in the street by young people who took pictures of me with the signed book.

There are as many different cultures in Asia as in Europe. Japan, being an archipelago, protects its traditions with fervour. Katsuyuki Tanaka is one of these dedicated guardians. He sits next to me at the end of lunch, asks to taste the twelve wines on offer, and eats quickly. He asks me a few questions, and before leaving an hour later, offers to pay me a visit in France as he is keen to taste and take part in a blending session. I find his request highly surprising. He sends me a message and decides to come over in January 2013. While I wonder about it, his visit piques my curiosity. We make an appointment at 8 in the morning to taste. We'll taste Château-Laville-Bertrou, whose vineyards are in the village of La Livinière, in the Minervois area. I hand over a glass to him and explain the stakes at play. Having exchanged a few sentences in Tokyo and nothing since, we are in a process of mutual discovery, and I have no doubt he'll surprise me during the morning. My team imposes a steady tasting rhythm. The aim is to put together the Le Viala blend, which comes from a registered plot where Syrah, Grenache, Carignan, and Mourvèdre are grown. Next, we'll attempt to blend the estate cuvée. I feel very quickly that Mr Tanaka needs to proceed at his own pace. I watch his reactions and do not ask any questions. I prefer these minimalist exchanges as blending requires concentration and feeling.

I watch carefully this man who arrived the day before from Japan and about whom I know almost nothing. He closes his eyes and brings his left index finger to the glass. Time stops. I ask myself what he is doing, and, as I dare not ask, I assume he is looking for the wine's vibration. A few seconds later, he takes drawing paper and coloured pencils from his satchel. As the tasting proceeds, he starts drawing curves. We continue working, and I suggest to Ghislain that we each attempt a blend of the Viala. We are not too far from the harmony and balance we seek. We try four different blends, 0.5% different from each other. The difference between them is noticeable as soon as one of the components change.

2012 is an odd vintage, rather good in the Languedoc, whereas the Rhône Valley was plagued by floods. We consult our guest on the final decision. Blending wines from four small plots from the same place is often trickier than working with

Blending wines from four small plots from the same place is often trickier than working with many plots

many plots. We all agree that the third blend is the most successful one. The wine is distinguished, elegant, complex, and in line with those of previous vintages. Katsuyuki asks for the proportion of the blend, and I give him the figures: Syrah 59%, Grenache 23%, Carignan 11%, Mourvèdre 7%, nothing out of the ordinary for us.

He pauses and then says in perfect English, “Do you realise you’ve only used prime numbers?” I stop in my tracks. This alchemy has been arrived at by the same process as a thousand previous ones, but I don’t yet realise that this moment will change the way I blend wines.

Katsuyuki Tanaka was born in Japan. He forged his own path, which is rare enough to be pointed out. After completing his studies, he left for New York, where he worked as a chef, developing his knowledge of Western culture and his understanding of international cuisine. He also explored spirituality, especially Christian transcendence. Back in Japan, he started learning as much as he could about wines. His vision of the world, people, wines and terroirs is, however, truly different. He’s developed a specific form of supra sensitivity and connection with others that can be puzzling.

The following Saturday, I invited him for lunch at my family home on the Cigalus estate. My wife, Ingrid, asked me what the plan was. I told her we’d both go to the Narbonne market as Tanaka had offered to cook for us. The Narbonne market, recently voted the best in France, is a colourful place where people go to meet as well as drink a coffee, have a glass of wine or comment on the latest Racing rugby game. We bought a Mediterranean sea bass and fresh pasta. When he arrived at our place, Katsuyuki greeted Ingrid and our children, Emma and Mathias, and insisted he be left alone in the kitchen and not disturbed. He checked with me the different salts at our disposal and chose the Gruissan salt flower. Before he started to cook, he told me that sea salt should only be used when cooking fish and hornless animals such as pork, and mountain salt for beef and horned animals. The latter are connected to the cosmos and their meat needs high-altitude salt that enhances flavours and sublimates them. Try it when cooking meat: prepare half with sea salt and half with mountain salt. The difference is amazing. Despite Katsuyuki's instructions, I couldn't resist going back to the kitchen and observing the way he gutted the fish and put it in the oven, as well as the care he took over cooking temperatures. The meal is delicious. We drink a 2015 white Cigalus, voted best airline business class white wine at the Cellar in the Sky competition, a first for Air France and a source of great pride for us. In the middle of the meal, Katsuyuki leaves the table and disappears for half an hour. We assume he must have gone for a wander in the vineyard. He comes back without giving an explanation and finishes the meal with a smile on his face. In the living room, we drink a small glass of 1959 Rivesaltes, and he starts asking me questions about biodynamics and the notion of terroir. I am truly impressed, not just by his knowledge of the great vineyards of the world but also by his impressive knowledge of Languedoc terroirs.

I am pleased with this first meeting, which marks the beginning of several visits and blending sessions, the last one being in 2019. We discussed many topics such as the meaning of life, spirituality, the role of wine in Japan and in the world. I invited him to visit several of our projects. He taught me about stone polarity and his vision of the circulation of energies in a room or cellar. The location of the new Clos du Temple cellar also prompted many discussions.

I introduced him to my wine friends. We tasted together with Marc and Mathieu Dubernet, Jean-Claude Berrouet, but also Rick Garced, the Founding president & CEO of the United States Sommelier Association. Over two to three meetings a year, we developed esteem and great respect for each other. During the Covid era, which was very long and hard in a big city such as Tokyo, I took part at his request in several online conferences with his students. I am looking forward to his next visit. This exceptional man entered my life thanks to the grace of God, and I thank him for sharing timeless moments with me.

CHAPTER 3

THE QUEST FOR MEANING

The spirit of conquest

Over thirty years, I built a unique portfolio of exceptional vineyards and terroirs. The reasons for this frenetic buying spree are threefold. My parents taught me good work ethics and a sense of responsibility from a very young age. At sixteen, I was the winemaker at the Domaine de Villemajou. I used to miss two weeks of school to help my father, working night and day. Rugby also made me hold myself to higher standards, developed my spirit of conquest, and firmed up my desire to compete with the best in all circumstances.

From 1987, the date of my official start in the profession, to 1995 when I bought the Cigalus estate, I took time to learn, travel, and meet people. At thirty, I took up the challenge of taking over Villemajou, keeping it as Georges intended while giving it a new dimension. I ended a successful rugby career after winning the Yves du Manoir challenge three times with my Narbonne friends and competing with the best teams in the country. The last season at Stade Français was an amazing experience and provided me with a smooth transition towards my new responsibilities. Meeting Max

Guazzini, the pioneering chairman of this centenary club, opened my eyes to the desire to be bold and disruptive.

The company grew over thirty years from ten to four hundred and fifty employees. This fascinating human adventure was built the hard-earned way, with the conviction that nothing is impossible. My desire to create a constellation of estates is linked to my visceral need to create and position our region on the map of the world's wines. Each purchase answered a common denominator: a fascination, first for the terroir, often for the landscapes, and sometimes for the architecture or history of a place.

My desire to create a constellation of estates is linked to my visceral need to create and position our region on the map of the world's wines.

I was a wine broker at the beginning of my career. The Divimer (Diffusion des Vins Méditerranéens) brokerage firm was founded by my father in the 1970s. The job was to sell wine in bulk, mostly to regional wine merchants. Later, we supplied prestigious clients such as Nicolas wine shops in Paris. The job of a wine broker is demanding. You need to collect samples and negotiate with producers and wine merchants. The market can shrink according to many parameters linked to available quantities and wine quality. The 1970s-1980s were still the glory era for table wines, which were still more part of the daily diet than occasional treats. France was an agricultural country, and hard work was the norm. French peasants used to drink wine from breakfast onwards, and bars served white or red wines by the glass at the counter.

A hundred and twenty litres per year per head wasn't enough to quench the thirst of French people. They were not drunkards, but their lifestyle and social life were very different from what they are nowadays. Not every house had a television or a phone. Life was slow. The Thirty Glorious Years, the constant rise in living standards, and social progress created a sense of harmony and well-being in society. It was the same in Italy, Spain, or Portugal. France, which was ahead in economic terms, was an aspirational model for these southern countries.

The social and cultural life of wine was part of our lifestyle. Bordeaux wines hadn't undergone the development and price appreciation that was to follow. Some Grands Crus were still shipped in barrels and bottled in Belgium, Holland, or the United Kingdom. Luxury and marketing codes hadn't entered the world of wine.

There were several hundred wine merchants in the Languedoc. Wines were shipped mostly by rail in six-hundred hectolitre wagons. Rosé appeared in the 1980s and only became popular ten years later thanks to the arrival of refrigeration appliances that allowed temperature-controlled winemaking to preserve aromas and avoid oxidation.

It was in this lively environment that I started my career. The Languedoc used to produce over twenty million hectolitres a year, and imported wines from Italy, Spain, and Algeria to improve the colour and alcoholic strength of local wines. Life was easy, and people used to think their children would have a better future. This prevailing optimism encouraged social interaction and public life.

I used to taste two hundred wines per day with my teammate Henri Roig, using the notebooks and scoring systems tried and tested by my father. Henri was a Catalan and worked by my side for ten years. We were so aligned that it was as if our two palates were one. We liked the same wines and enjoyed tasting together enormously. He hailed from the Roussillon, which was still a huge wine-producing area in the 1990s, with the bonus of producing seven hundred thousand hectolitres of *vins doux naturels.* I always had a soft spot for these wines as they had a strong taste identity and a charming sweetness derived from the main grape variety of the region. Noir, Gris, or White Grenache are well suited to the Mediterranean climate as they can cope with the summer drought and are naturally full-bodied with an elegant tannic structure. Through ageing in wooden vats, barrels, glass jars, or cement vats, these wines develop a unique aromatic complexity over time.

Travelling over the Languedoc and Roussillon day after day made me discover the hinterlands of Faugères, Maury, or Estagel where wines are stronger and more powerful. On the gentle slopes of the Mediterranean coast, wines are fresher and more seductive. I've always had a soft spot for the dry white wines of Collioure, made from Grenache Gris and Macabeu. There, the same plot can produce *vins doux naturels* or precise, taut dry white wines that display the minerality of the terroir. My favourite producers are located at the foothills of the Pyrenees as they produce characterful wines. Castelmaure in Corbières, Cascastel in Fitou, and Tautavel in the Roussillon produce wines that resemble the local winegrowers, colourful and a bit rebellious.

My job taught me that business is discussed around a restaurant table and that decisions are made before cheese is served. My rugby career with the Narbonne team facilitated local relationships and created instant bonds. My determination and my loyalty did the rest. I was a wine broker from Monday to Thursday, a winegrower on Friday and Saturday, and I played rugby on Sundays. It meant that, apart from a few wild nights in Narbonne on those Sundays when my team won a game, I lived like a monk. My life was intensely busy and full.

It took me a long time to understand the reasons for my commitment: education, family history, and my father's drive all added to my natural fieriness and impetuous character. I met every single important local decision-maker and sometimes benefited from their considerate protection and support. Yves Barsalou, my neighbour in Bizanet and a guardian figure, was the chairman of the National Fund of the Crédit Agricole bank. He authorised my first investments and followed my professional beginnings. Robert Skalli and Bernard Jeanjean, well-established wine merchants; the Bonfils brothers in Sète; and Bernard Péré-Lahaille in Carcassonne extended the hand of friendship to me. I never took advantage and always respected them while protecting my independence.

To be as ambitious as I was in the Languedoc required great secrecy. I only began to share my vision for the region after buying Château l'Hospitalet in 2002. After fifteen years in the profession, I was ready to compete with the best wines in the world. My battle plan was quasi-military: conquer the French market first, then Europe and the world. This plan was implemented at the same time as we were switching our vineyards to biodynamic practices, improving the quality of our wines, and building a dedicated and close-knit team. Stéphane Durand and Éric Lacombe were the first to join me. Their energy and winner mentality were contagious. I shared with my team the motto of Che Guevara, who was neither a tradesman nor a philosopher but a warrior fighting for a utopia: "Be realistic, demand the impossible."

For twenty-five years we built a solid bedrock and a team of adventurers, creating a group that grew in strength with time. We didn't earn any money, but we were paying our debts and growing.

As no importer was keen to represent me in the United States, I decided to create an importing company and visit distributors and direct clients myself. The trust put in me by the Southern Glazer's Wine and Spirits group, as well as some independent distributors such as MS Walker or United, has propelled our company into another dimension. I spent ten weeks a year over ten years in the United States. I made firm friends and got to know the market and its complexity state by state. Arriving at the right time with a range of rosé wines well-suited to the needs of the market gave us a competitive edge. The American dream is within reach of those who share this conquering spirit. We became the leading brand of French wine there.

The strength of our brands and our DNA rests on irreproachable quality, a carefully thought-out segmentation and hierarchy, and a well-thought-out conquest plan. Our marketing, data, and communication investments were as sizeable as the challenges ahead. My teams knew how to anticipate the market's needs and create the brands consumers wanted.

My job as a conductor is engrossing. Managing, training, and inspiring teams as well as ensuring the quality of the wines is an exhilarating task. The development of the client's experience offers wine drinkers the opportunity to live and experiment with the values of the company, enjoy the food and wine matches in our restaurants, and take part in masterclasses. Every year the jazz festival at Château l'Hospitalet offers an immersive experience linking music, wines, gastronomy, and culture.

Managing, training, and inspiring teams as well as ensuring the quality of the wines is an exhilarating task.

The philosophy of action

Existential questions about the meaning of life are a frequent occurrence. It is normal to sometimes feel low when contemplating the infinite field of potentialities and understanding the temporal, intellectual, and energetic limits of human life. There are several billion galaxies in the universe. Current advances in astrophysics and quantum science challenge our understanding of the world. Science and mathematics are thwarted by Planck's wall, the limit of the knowledge of the universe, named after the German physicist Max Planck, and cannot fully explain the Big Bang theory. We remain dazzled by celestial and earthly structures.

It took several thousand years, from Australopithecus to the Neolithic era, for mankind to believe in the immortality of the soul. Sedentary lifestyles and the development of agriculture fostered the evolution of Neanderthals into Homo sapiens. The Palaeolithic rock art discovered in grottos and caves, mostly featuring animals, depicts the hunting and gathering lifestyle of the time while giving a glimpse of transcendental aspirations. Animism entails the belief that all living things, as well as nature itself, have a soul and a life force. Shamans in various civilisations have linked the earthly world with the invisible. Their role is to heal, improve the lives of communities, protect them, and bring rain, good harvests, and plentiful hunting.

The development of mankind and the invention of writing contributed to a spiritual and transcendental blossoming and a cognitive revolution. The prophet Abraham played a central part in the creation of religions. In Greece, polytheism organised the life of cities. Philosophy was born and encouraged the disciples of Socrates, the great master, to propagate his message of a virtuous and temperate life, doing good and being wise. Plato took it further, opposing the world of sensations to the world of reason. He stated that death frees the soul and believed in God, contrary to Epicurus, who was materialistic and thought that the quest for pleasure was the goal of life. Fulfilling simple pleasures such as drinking, eating, and sleeping, and the absence of worries linked to self-knowledge, is the cornerstone of Greek philosophy. Aristotle agreed with Plato and Epicurus on the conception of happiness. He stated that reason is empty before the senses kick in. "It is by their character that men are what they are, but it is by their actions that they are either happy or not."

The story of the Hebrew people, the power of Greek philosophy, spiritual movements in India, and Confucianism in China have, in the same era, established the fundamental basis of modern life and created a link between the East and the West. Transcendental thinking, whether linked or not to the survival of the soul and therefore immortality, places us in a unique situation and questions the meaning of our lives and our freedom to choose. Action frees us from the limitations of the finiteness of human life and puts into motion our thoughts, ideas, and needs.

The art of living

Situated between the infinitely large (macrocosm) and the infinitely small (microcosm), we try to find meaning in our lives. Education, learning, studies, sport, entertainment, and more recently, the virtual world, feed our thoughts, create a social corpus, and engender emotions. All this information is filtered by the various states of our conscience, fostering the development of our personality and giving birth to a unique human being. Each of us must find our path to flourish while ranking our priorities. This experience, which can happen at different stages of life, according to our life and its conditions, will allow us to choose our ambitions, be they personal or professional.

"Man must act as much as possible, and existence is essentially action," said Gottfried Wilhelm Leibniz.

Action frees you. It creates movement and encourages reasoning. For Leibniz, nothing is without reason; otherwise, the world would be absurd. From birth, we are trapped in a process, suffered or desired in turns, creating consequences and influencing our life. Life consists of efforts and sacrifices that justify actions as well as interactions with others and nature.

The strength of character of my grandmother, Paule Bertrand, was in this respect exceptional. Born on 1 January 1900, she lived through the last century, sharing with her large family and loved ones her moral and spiritual convictions and her unbreakable willpower. She had to face the loss of her parents as a teenager, take on the responsibility of looking after her younger brother, and, a few years later, cope with the loss of her first husband. She always faced adversity with courage, strength, and tenacity, first to build up her identity, then to start a family after living through the First World War in fear and uncertainty about the future.

Bringing up nine children on the low income derived from a two-and-a-half-hectare vineyard wasn't an easy task. Everything she did was inspired by her own philosophy and beliefs. Starting a family, implementing rules for living, and preparing children to find their way in a difficult world required a rarely found mental strength. Her life story is the cornerstone of my family, built upon a bedrock of hard work, courage, abnegation, and hope for a better future.

Her life story is the cornerstone of my family, built upon a bedrock of hard work, courage, abnegation, and hope for a better future.

Later, my father Georges decided to create his own future, one that met his expectations as a rugby player, referee, and winegrower. With my mother, Geneviève, he climbed the ladder of regional representativity aiming for two goals: first, building a coherent and structured wine estate, and then raising the quality and image of the wines of our region.

These two lives have marked my childhood, shaped my teenage years, and prepared me to explore my own path. Demanding vineyard work during the school holidays and the discipline, leadership, and team spirit of my rugby club developed my abilities and willpower far more than my rather modest academic achievements. This demanding training didn't diminish my deep desires; on the contrary, it acted as an accelerator. Confidence fosters action and decision-making. My natural yearning for the sacred and spiritual, by giving legitimacy to my ambition, has given strength to my childhood dreams and helped me envision my future path. I always dreamt big and was never thwarted. My parents encouraged me to play a lot of sports and pursue my passion for rugby. I was determined to have a career as a rugby player at the highest level. Despite a few setbacks and injuries to start with, my strength, willpower, and technique helped me to reach the top and play for ten years in the first division. As rugby wasn't yet a professional sport, I was able to develop my wine knowledge and abilities at the same time.

In 1987, aged twenty-two, I took over the family company, determined to make a name for myself. I worked very hard to build a reputation faithful to the memory of my father's demanding talent. Once I had built that trust and a circle of loyal friends and advisors, I climbed to the top of the local wine world, one step at a time, with my eyes always on an even bigger goal. Rugby gave me the necessary strength, energy, and spirit of conquest to fulfil my destiny. What was once only my job would become my mission statement. I still had many surprises in store.

Once you've got started and have earned the necessary legitimacy to achieve your task, you're propelled by an irresistible force that helps you step up and clarify the decisions that need to be made. Sometimes luck intervenes, enabling you to meet new people and paving the way while opening new doors and new horizons. My professional, but also personal growth, was an obstacle course during the first twenty years of my career. To start with, I made my lives as a rugby player and a winegrower coexist.

Weekdays were for work and weekends for rugby games. It took structure, discipline, and a lot of energy. My dreams of sporting glory forged my desire to surpass myself and succeed with my teammates to win titles, entertain supporters, and, beyond that, contribute to the legend of the Narbonne club and the greatness of the city. This era fed my hunger for conquest and strengthened the beliefs I was developing in my life as a winegrower.

It took me over twenty years to go from critical to commercial success and ten more years to create a worldwide brand. The pain caused by failures strengthened my drive to achieve success. A quick decision-maker, always on the move and always listening to my inner voice, my creativity and desire to innovate were often guided by my fertile imagination. The art of living is a concept I developed as the thread that runs through everything I do. It encompasses the millennia-old history of our region with its cultural and gastronomical traditions. To be the ambassador of this Mediterranean culture gives meaning to my life every day and gives me the freedom to create and raise the quality of our wines and our terroirs. History was on the march. It was only a question of time and patience.

Prime numbers

After blending the Viala wine, my guest of the day, Katsuyuki Tanaka, pointed out that all the proportions we'd used were prime numbers. This comment marked an important turning point in my approach to blending. First, I studied the properties of numbers, their use in life, and their importance in nature. It is fascinating to understand better the structure of the universe, the five Platonic solids*, sacred geometry, and perspectives. Euclid, a mathematician from ancient Greece, demonstrated the power of the relationship between numbers. Egyptians built pyramids, including Khufu's, and the Romans, inspired by the Greeks, built the Pantheon using the golden ratio. In the 18th century, the Italian mathematician Leonardo Fibonacci discovered the sequence of numbers named after him: 1, 2, 3, 5, 8, 13, and so on to infinity, with the ratio of successive numbers approaching the golden ratio, 1.61803. This golden ratio was used by the greatest architects, scholars, and Renaissance painters to express perfection, perspective, and harmony. Leonardo da Vinci, in his drawing of the Vitruvian Man, represents a perfectly structured human body according to the golden ratio. It is striking to realise that many plants in nature are organised according to the same ratio. The Fibonacci sequence can be found in pinecones, sunflowers, passion flowers, cabbages, and starfish. Everything in nature is based on numbers and is perfectly structured.

When blending wines, I often noticed that a fifty-fifty or

---

* The tetrahedron, octahedron, cube, icosahedron, and dodecahedron.

eighty-twenty ratio never created harmony, whereas the use of eighty-three-seventeen or seventy-one-twenty-nine would create balance. Using three, four, or five components, I realised that the more prime numbers I used, the better the results. I tried and tested this mathematical approach with my teams. Applying this theory doesn't replace tasting, analysis, and method, but it helps to pave the way and save time among the infinite field of possibilities.

Achieving the most balanced blend, magnifying the expression of terroir, requires asceticism and a long process of internalisation, deep feelings, and connections. Some sportsmen talk about the flow, this elusive moment when you feel both fulfilment and an acute awareness of uber-sensitivity. At that time, performance is enhanced. This quest for sensations is the way to follow to achieve the perfect blend. It delivers a harmonious feeling of verticality, depth, and length on the palate. Out of a hundred, I'll always use three or four prime number percentages. When I first became aware of prime numbers, and for a few years afterwards, we always compared these blends

Achieving the most balanced blend, magnifying the expression of terroir, requires asceticism and a long process of internalisation, deep feelings, and connections. Some sportsmen talk about the flow, this elusive moment when you feel both fulfilment and an acute awareness of uber-sensitivity.

blind, not to be prejudiced, with others made with different ratios to validate our approach objectively. This innovative approach brought us closer to the great Renaissance painters who used the golden square and rectangle to structure their paintings. If everything in nature is based on the golden ratio, it would be a pity not to use this rule to better express the secrets of a vintage, without dogmatism.

The wine blender has the talent, know-how, and experience. He follows his intuitions and flashes of inspiration within a set framework. Constraints include the grape varieties planted on the estate, the blend proportions of previous vintages, and the desire to seek balance and the true expression of a vintage. Every vintage has its own specificities, linked to the climate, the timing of flowering, fruit set, and *véraison*, and how ripening progressed. This identity card for the year can be not only revealed but also sublimated by human genius.

To give meaning to raw material and understand the aim of the task means digging deep within oneself for the ability to deliver a unique vibration. Prime numbers are no guarantee of a successful blend, if only because of the high number of combinations resting on this mathematical premise. Once the stakes and the major components at play have been identified, exploration and creativity can kick in. Freestyle is pointless without a framework. Rigour and methodology are prerequisites; organisation gets the ball rolling, and creativity transcends the whole exercise. This initiatory path creates the perfect conditions for ecstasy and deep joy.

Each professional has their own routine, preliminary steps, and specific vocabulary. Some work in a more rational manner.

Left-brain thinkers are more analytical and methodical. Right-brain thinkers, often more intuitive, have flashes of inspiration. I try, in my own way, to combine both to achieve the most accomplished creation and the most authentic and expressive wine. We are all seeking the perfect ratio, the one that will reveal the hidden treasures of an estate.

A successful blend will be an improvement on all single wines from the estate taken individually. Anything can be added or taken away, but it is essential to find the cornerstone, the spine on which all individual wines will rest to create the final blend. It is very often the same so-called reference plots that will protect and best express the origin, typicity, and character of a terroir from one vintage to the next.

As with the building of a temple, the work starts with the foundations, then the columns, walls, intermediary structures, and finally the roof. Depending on the estate, the grape varieties, and the soil structure, the approach will be different. A great wine is put together for the long term; it will improve for decades. The pure expression of the terroir is sought, without artifices. What matters is the unique and distinctive character of each constituent wine and their complementarity. There are sometimes charming wines that play solo. They're called fake friends or troublemakers. They have too much of a tannic structure and irreconcilable asperities.

A successful blend is like a sports team in which everyone finds their place. One per cent more or less of a wine or grape variety can change the final blend. It can sometimes be as little as 0.1%, and although it won't change the aromas, it will change perception on the palate. This is true for all wine colours: white, rosé, red, and

A great wine will reveal the soul of the place, its history, and its surrounding ecosystem. Grapes absorb aromas from the surrounding flora and capture both the aromatic spectrum of fruit, flowers, and roots and their telluric and cosmic energy.

orange. For the latter, the aim is to find a balance between the tannins and the fat of the wine. It is the tension between minerality and body for white wines. A great wine will reveal the soul of the place, its history, and its surrounding ecosystem. Grapes absorb aromas from the surrounding flora and capture both the aromatic spectrum of fruit, flowers, and roots and their telluric and cosmic energy.

Plant-based – orchids, chamomile – biodynamic preparations as well as sprays of oak bark will prevent or cure vine diseases. Silica reinforces rigour and vitality. A living wine offers a sensory experience.

The shape of a tank or bottle can also influence the energy of a wine and how it will keep. The Clos du Temple bottle was designed using the golden ratio. The objective was to create a connection between telluric and cosmic forces, thus magnifying the wine.

The use of prime numbers allowed us to gain precision and efficiency. Beyond identifying, within an estate, the referent plot that will become the master beam of the final blend, the main question is the choice of the percentage of the complementary parts, those that will contribute complexity, tension, and depth to the wine. Often, the final decision rests on minority components that will bring the wine into another dimension. It is in this respect that adding 5, 7, or 11% instead of 4, 6, or 10% becomes meaningful.

This method of final selection has been tried and tested by my teams and works in 90% of cases. Sometimes, but rarely, another version may be preferred. The high standards to which we hold ourselves and the strong bond within the team guarantee real objectivity. If I feel we are unsure, I ask the other tasters to write their answers on a piece of paper to avoid influencing their choices, and if we do not agree, we start again on another day. There is no time limit to our search for excellence, only the result matters.

Once the barrels have been racked and blended into vats, we let the wine rest, and we carry out laboratory analysis to decide if the wine needs to be fined with organic egg whites. Nothing is systematic in our way of working; each vintage will find its truth. Ghislain Coux, my alter ego, assisted by Charmian Moulin, a talented oenologist, always contributes to our operational excellence with his rigour and winemaking and tasting talent. Bottling will only take place on a flower or fruit day, according to the lunar calendar, after a minimum of two to three months ageing in barrels. After bottling, the wines are stored in our temperature-controlled warehouses for a minimum of six months and sometimes for several years before shipping. My father said to me many times when I was young, "You know, Gérard, wine is made of thousands of details."

Amen.

Inspiring viticulture

Living soils capture and retain more carbon than trees. Soil humidification requires careful management of biomass, microbial action, and the limitation or suppression of nitrogen or potash fertilisers and synthetic products. Viticulture, because of its symbolic rather than vital dimension, could serve as an example and inspire the rest of agriculture. We have tested a transition process to biological and biodynamic agriculture which provides proven solutions and protects the quality of soils and subsoils. While studying this process, INRAE (France's National Research Institute for Agriculture, Food, and Environment), Food, and Environment, made a surprising discovery. The number of links between micro-organisms and soil bacteria changes according to the type of agriculture from 1,000 links in conventional agriculture, to 1,500 in organic agriculture and 47,000 in soils cultivated biodynamically! The positive consequence of the improvement in soil life is the growth of organic matter. A 1% increase results in the storage of 31.5 tonnes more carbon per hectare. These figures are impressive and represent a significant source of hope. The same is true for woods and forests, which act as carbon sinks. Combined actions from

The number of links between micro-organisms and soil bacteria changes according to the type of agriculture from 1,000 links in conventional agriculture, to 1,500 in organic agriculture and 47,000 in soils cultivated biodynamically!

agriculture and forestry at different levels will allow for significant improvement.

Water management is a real challenge for humanity. It is a global issue that will require not only a geopolitical and multipronged strategy to ensure that dams creating resources for some do not create deserts for others, but also daring innovations to capture rainwater and store it for use throughout the year. The challenge consists in using river water cautiously and, if necessary, subterranean water, while ensuring the volume taken isn't more than can be replenished in the water table. There will be no economic development nor ecological improvement without a reliable and continuous water supply. Water management has become a priority for many countries and regions. Viticulture will not avoid this issue, especially in semi-arid areas. Water will become more expensive but should remain available for inhabitants, the environment, agriculture, industry, and tourism. Its management is a long-term political challenge that requires quick, far-sighted decisions everywhere on earth. Water is also crucial for maintaining humid soils and thus for storing carbon globally. Water is as important as the air we breathe or the sun that creates the prerequisites for life on earth. Water, air, and sunlight are three sacred and universal resources, fundamentals that should be managed without territorial bias. Resource distribution and management are the main issues that need to be resolved. Great visionaries, from the Middle Ages onwards, have thought out and integrated water needs according to the seasons in supply channels. In the South of France, Philippe Lamour created the Bas-Rhône-Languedoc canal in the 1950s, collecting water by way of Alpine melting snow from the Rhône River and its tributaries. In the Pyrenees, the Vinça dam on the Têt river, built in 1976, improved water supply to the Roussillon plain.

California, Arizona, and Nevada are facing a perfect storm of drought, population growth, and poor resource management. These three states wouldn't have experienced the same development over the last eighty years without the creation of Lake Mead in 1936, which provided them with a large water storage facility, enabling them to store water from the heavy rains in 2023.

It takes political courage to undertake huge investments that will only pay off over several generations. Water is currently priced very reasonably, especially for agriculture and industry, protecting their yields and business models. Sobriety is a different concept from limitation: the former allows efficacy, efficiency, and autonomy, while the latter creates barriers and frustrations, generating anger and desires for new horizons.

Water issues cannot remain political, left to the decisions of minorities. Water is life, and there will be no agricultural, touristic, or economic development if it becomes scarce. Rainfall patterns on earth are changing, and the increasing frequency of extreme weather events such as hurricanes and typhoons disrupt our centuries-old systems. Tomorrow's agriculture and food sovereignty will require anticipation of water needs, especially during the summer, for better management of river resources, development of storage areas, recovery of rainwater, and re-use of wastewater. In Southern European countries, especially in the south of France, water is plentiful enough to be managed better. The Mediterranean basin requires structural investments that will create wealth, guarantee biodiversity, and combat desertification and forest fires. It is therefore urgent, wherever possible, to reverse the trend of inaction and create a virtuous action plan around water, which is as precious as the air we breathe and should remain a resource available in a set framework, ensuring equal opportunities, the stability of ecosystems and populations, and fostering economic development.

Another issue on which we can take action concerns us: improving soil quality. In France and worldwide, soils are increasingly degraded due to the intensive use of chemicals. The biological destruction of soils, caused by the multiplication of inputs in intensive agriculture, has resulted in bacteria multiplying twenty times faster than fungi. This imbalance stops the production of humus and mineralises organic matter. Soils become poorer and lose their biotope, especially worms, which are key providers and keepers of magnesium, potassium, and nitrogen. This degradation contributes to erosion, which, whenever it rains, washes soil elements, particularly clay, into the sea. We lose on average, one centimetre of landmass per year in France. Cultivating soils organically and biodynamically to create a virtuous and resilient ecosystem and return to higher

We lose on average, one centimetre of landmass per year in France. Cultivating soils organically and biodynamically to create a virtuous and resilient ecosystem and return to higher levels of organic matter is a way to stop this soil degradation.

levels of organic matter is a way to stop this soil degradation.

There are numerous challenges ahead of us, which are fascinating. They require solidarity, exemplary leaders, and strong souls capable of resisting partisan pressures and lobbies.

CHAPTER 4

THE FOURTH DIMENSION

The art of celebration and sharing

The monks of the Saint-Hilaire Abbey, near Limoux in the Aude department, invented the first sparkling wine in 1531. The second fermentation of wine in the spring, caused by residual sugar, was likely a fortunate accident. Regardless of the circumstances, this miracle transformed social life at the time and inspired the monk Dom Pérignon, who introduced this vinification method to Champagne in the 17th century.

What a fantastic journey these bottles have taken, celebrating personal, professional, institutional, social, sports, and family-related occasions! It took us time to understand and master the production process, particularly in maintaining the pressure within bottles. Four bars of pressure represent considerable strength and energy, released upon opening, creating billions of bubbles in a glass.

Blanquette de Limoux and its typical grape variety, Mauzac, claim the origin of this know-how, which was later refined by the monks of Champagne through the process known as the traditional method or Champagne method. This included mastering the second fermentation in the bottle and fostered a healthy rivalry among the legendary Champagne houses such as Krug, Veuve Clicquot, Moët & Chandon, Taittinger, Bollinger, Roederer, and later cooperatives like Nicolas Feuillatte. The blends, primarily from Chardonnay, Pinot Noir, and Pinot Meunier, have led to the development of various taste profiles. Maturation has enhanced aromas and complexity. The winegrowers of Sieur d'Arques in Limoux introduced Chardonnay and Pinot Noir to complement Chenin, producing well-crafted wines. The birth of Crémant in the main French wine-growing regions created a category that can compete with the best sparkling wines.

Cava in Spain, Franciacorta in Italy, also available as a traditional method, Prosecco, Spumante, and later, other sparkling wines from all wine-producing countries have generated considerable interest. Following brut and demi-sec, sparkling rosés appeared, adding diversity to the category. Some, especially in Russia and the USA, used the Champagne name for their wines for many years. International agreements have now put an end to this identity theft.

I have always liked sparkling wines, symbols of the festive spirit and the celebration of special moments with family and friends. Party time after a game is sacred in rugby. It is a fundamental part of our sport. Unlike our Anglo-Saxon friends who have established a tradition of drinking beer after a game, often starting in the changing rooms, I have always enjoyed introducing good wines to my friends and sharing them.

The podiums of Formula 1 Grands Prix have institutionalised the ritual of spraying competitors and the audience with champagne. Large formats like magnums are more fun and extend the ephemeral pleasure of these celebratory moments. Sommeliers and chefs love sabering bottles to immortalise an occasion. Sparkling wines represent joy, ecstasy, light-heartedness, and human fraternity.

Sparkling wines represent joy, ecstasy, light-heartedness, and human fraternity.

I started producing sparkling wines on a modest scale at the beginning of the 2000s, in partnership with Limoux winegrowers. As I lacked the know-how and equipment needed to produce sparkling wines, I surrounded myself with experts such as Alain Gayda, Jacques Delmas, Françoise Antech, and Michel Rosier, when tasting musts before fermentation to select the raw material for our brands. We began with the Thomas Jefferson cuvée, an homage to the American president who was a great admirer of Limoux wines. He discovered the area when he was the American ambassador to France.

I have been fortunate enough to have James Guillepain as a vice president for two years. James spent his life promoting Dom Pérignon and Moët & Chandon worldwide. This unconventional character led me into the world of champagne and explained his market conquest strategy, especially in Japan and the USA. His marketing approach and passion for excellence fascinated me. I discovered the concept of *plénitude* dear to Dom Pérignon and fell in love with the 2022 vintage, one of the greatest in my opinion, first when it was released and then in Plénitude 2, after more than fifteen years in the bottle. The perfect balance between minerality, aromatic complexity, freshness, and elegance is a masterpiece. It made me keen to get involved with sparkling wines. James introduced me to Philippe Coulon, one of the main architects of Moët et Chandon's rise to power and the launch of the Chandon know-how in various countries. I offered him a consulting position with our group. A former rugby player and now retired, he kindly agreed to assist us in our desire to develop high-quality Chardonnay and Pinot-based sparkling wines in Limoux. Assisted by the talented Jean Baptiste Terlay, we discovered a whole new world and had to completely reassess the markers of our still wine expertise. Harvesting dates, acidity, alcohol content, blending, everything was different. I love starting from a blank canvas and discovering a new work method. This is how, for five years, together, we blended Code Rouge and Ballerine, our two main cuvées, and aged Aigle Impérial to launch a premium wine aged horizontally for nine years. The international development of sparkling wine sales created the right market conditions for the launch of strong premium brands. After years of relative anonymity regarding our expertise, we invested in a dedicated cellar to mature, produce, and store our wines. The launch of a new 'brut nature' wine range called French Cancan, symbolic of the French spirit and evocative of a joyful, cheeky, and exuberant France, was a great motivation for us. It gave us the opportunity to introduce wine drinkers to a brut, an orange, and a rosé sparkling wine - a true innovation. The white is made from Chardonnay and Pinot, with a touch of Grenache Blanc as a terroir signature, the rosé from Pinot, Chardonnay, and Cinsault, and the orange from Chardonnay, Vermentino, and Viognier. All the grapes are organic.

I have been fortunate enough to work with a team ever ready to take on technical challenges. With Stéphane Queralt, Jean-Marie Lasmènes, Laurence Almin, Johan Censier, and Benoît Blancheton, we have a team of oenologists passionate about implementing new ideas.

Exploring new avenues, creating unprecedented experiences, this is the meaning of my life. Wine is a serious product that shouldn't take itself seriously. We are going to infuse the lives of our customers with joyous bubbles, creating universes and atmospheres true to the French spirit. Sparkling wines can be enjoyed anytime, on their own, or as a cocktail component. They are transgenerational wines that celebrate life's moments and the magic of the present. France, beyond the exalted status of champagne, must rise to the challenge of fulfilling the drinking needs of more casual occasions - drinks, pool parties, cocktails, evening parties - for a fresh take on celebration and partying.

From bubbles to show-business

The ambiance of cabarets has created a phantasmagorical universe best exemplified by the film Moulin Rouge: for one evening, the grind of daily life is forgotten and replaced by freedom and pleasure. France is the curator of this unique spirit, celebrated the world over, a vision that immortalises an art of living, bringing together figures such as Toulouse-Lautrec, Maurice Chevalier, Charles Trenet, Edith Piaf, Coco Chanel, Christian Dior, and Yves Saint-Laurent. Each, in their time, contributed to the cultural standing of our country and its terroirs, freeing a new energy, breaking codes, and launching trends. Paris, with its theatres, dance halls, restaurants, brasseries, and hotels, has epitomised this light-heartedness, elegance, and irresistible charm of our country and its people at their best.

I try to enjoy simple, joyful moments as much as big celebrations. Life is an experience that must be lived with intensity. I am always happy to take part in prestigious events, having had the privilege to be invited to the Cannes Festival, various Music Awards ceremonies, and, most recently, to the Élysée Palace by the president of the Republic to launch the Rugby World Cup with great French chefs. These unique moments propagate the image of an enthusiastic and radiant France, confident in its strengths.

The privilege of sharing a lunch with the two hundred best French chefs and *Meilleurs Ouvriers de France**, under the high patronage of Guillaume Gomez, French gastronomy ambassador to the world, spurs me to enjoy every moment. I love the camaraderie among chefs, their esprit de corps, and their fraternal drive to shine a light on culinary art.

Celebrating also means organising large events throughout the year at Château l'Hospitalet, our main estate, at our other estates, or at our beach club, following the tradition of party spirit and love of our country. I also love partying at local celebrations, such as the one that celebrated the title of French champion of my beloved Corbières 15 club. From the initial whistle until the

---

*Meilleur Ouvrier de France, commonly called MOF, means "best craftsman of France" and it is a title that is awarded to the best of the best. The concept was created in 1924, as a way to preserve and promote traditional crafts. There are now more than 200 categories of awards for more than 180 professions including pastry making and cheese making, stained glass and violin making, book binding and boot making, hairdressing and denture making.

middle of the night, we opened many bottles of Code Rouge and Ballerine. It was a beautiful and deeply moving celebration.

On a more personal level, I was honoured to be chosen to carry the Olympic Torch in 2024. It gave me an intense feeling of fulfilment and gratitude towards the world of sport and life-enhancing wine.

Encounters have punctuated my life. Artists, winegrowers, sportsmen, and international ambassadors have nourished my personal and professional life.

Encounters have punctuated my life. Artists, winegrowers, sportsmen, and international ambassadors have nourished my personal and professional life.

In April 2016, Katia Daguet Alonso, my assistant, told me, "You have a call from Jon Bon Jovi." I thought it was a prank. I picked up the phone, and Jon Bon Jovi, the global superstar, was indeed on the line. I soon understood why he was calling. He told me he loved wine, especially rosé, nicknamed pink juice in the USA, and that he loved to drink rosé in the Hamptons in the summer. Brad Vassar, who ran Southern Glazer's Wine & Spirits, our American importer and distributor, for over twenty years, had recommended me to him. Jon said he would like to launch a brand of rosé wine with his son Jesse and would like to meet me to explore the idea. We agreed to meet at the Saint Regis hotel in New York, with Irving Azoff, one of the most powerful men in the music industry, head of Live Nation, and Jon's friend and advisor since the beginning of his career. We talked for two hours with our respective lawyers and Steve Slatter, Executive Vice president and General Manager of the Wine Division of our shared distributor. Jon's sincerity, long-term vision, and professionalism impressed me. I understood the interest of developing a partnership and of launching a rosé to complement our existing brands. After agreeing to talk, I discovered over the following weeks how show business works in the USA, especially in terms of contracts. Our lawyers spent hours writing a memorandum of agreement before finalising the deal.

We quickly agreed on a shared vision and a clear launching strategy for this rosé, which we called Hampton Water. I invited my new partners to visit me in the Languedoc to discover the region and our group. It was the end of November 2017. They arrived in Narbonne and settled in at Château l'Hospitalet. We spent a lot of time working on the brand and its action plan. I quickly understood why Jon has been a star for forty years in the music world. Like a high-level sportsman or a successful entrepreneur, he has very high expectations. We share an attention to detail. I told him how we became the first French wine brand in the USA in ten years, as well as my vision for our product to be successful. Over the four days we spent together, having established a good rapport, we visited several estates. On the second evening, I invited them for dinner at the Auberge du Vieux Puits, Gilles Goujon's three-star Michelin restaurant in Fontjoncouse. This is an indispensable ritual for any celebrity staying in the Aude department. We drank a glass of our most popular rosé in the USA. "This is unreal", Jon said. "This village is a hidden jewel". He was utterly taken by the place, Mediterranean cooking, and the brilliant welcome from the chef.

The third day of his visit was the crucial one, as it was both the reason for him being there and when we would seal our joint endeavour. We were to meet at 8:30 am to blend our rosé. I arrived an hour earlier to check everything was in place. We had twenty samples representative of the Languedoc AOP, some vinified in barrels, including four different grape varieties: Grenache, Cinsault, Syrah, and Mourvèdre. The temperature was set at 19°C. Jon and Jesse arrived. The bottles, all with pink glass stoppers, were perfectly lined up, ten centimetres apart. Small details are part of the ceremonial. We were in the seduction and getting-to-know-each-other phase. I explained the rules of the game and handed a tasting notebook in English to my guests. It was their first professional tasting and blending. The tension was palpable. Jon asked me a few questions, and we got started. We benchmarked on the first three samples. Concentration was at its peak. Each time we moved on to a different grape variety, I announced the specificities of the wine and the way it was made or matured. An hour later, after tasting all twenty samples, we took a fifteen-minute break and exchanged impressions. My original idea, my conceptual approach was to create a rock 'n' roll rosé. There's no official guide for that, but the idea was to have a showy wine with edges, a portrayal of the rock attitude as seen in Jon's hits such as *It's My Life* or *Bed of Rosés.* Jon and Jesse wanted a high-quality rosé. The best way to proceed was for each of us to do our own initial blend and compare them. Jon impressed me with his depth of feelings and the precision of his approach. He and his son had instinctively used all four grape varieties, with

Jesse using a higher proportion of Mourvèdre. Once we compared our three blends, I took the lead. The aim was to create a premium rosé, sold at over $20 a bottle in the USA and around 15€ in France, setting a high standard. It was important for me to create a unique wine that would mirror our different temperaments, the music of wine, and the Franco-American friendship, from Marquis de Lafayette to today, not forgetting both World Wars.

Jesse, aged twenty-two, was discovering the world of wine and business. Jon, very involved, listened to each piece of advice. He was obviously enjoying the experience. We created a new rosé in the same way he composes a new song. He starts in the intimacy of his studio before launching an album whose success the audience will decide upon. You can plan, but you'll only know five years later if the song or the wine have found their fans and if the initial intention was correct.

It was our first collaboration. This novel experience was full of learning and taught me to compose, in all senses of the term, in a different way. A beautiful friendship was born between us, out of respect, work, and loyalty. A stronger bond would be born, year after year, as we have created something together that is bigger than us. Jon often says during press conferences,"Of all the French regions I know, Languedoc is the one with the best kept secrets." Our international distribution network allowed us to sell our brand in over fifty countries. Beyond our friendship and family get-togethers, we've learned from our respective different universes and lifestyles.

The *Festival Jazz à l'Hospitalet* allowed me to meet wonderful people. Yuri Buenaventura from Colombia, the salsa king, felt the energy of the place on his first evening there and decided to perform in the middle of the vineyard. His unique musicality and sense of rhythm worked wonders. Having become a favourite of the Narbonne audience, he treats us to great moments of emotion whenever he visits. After performing, he likes to share a drink during the evening session and mix with the audience to commune and share his exuberance and Latin sensitivity. One evening, we stayed up until five o'clock in the morning, sitting in a circle with Claude Spanghero* and a few friends, giving thanks to life and friendship between people. We were inebriated, happy in this timeless and surreal moment. Yuri is a rare friend, a lover of France and its culture and lifestyle. In his honour, we have planted an olive tree, as a symbol of peace and fraternity.

Jamie Cullum is the personification of jazz. His stage presence is unbelievable, his voice unique, and his generosity boundless. He spins around on stage and draws you into his own world. His performance at l'Hospitalet remains one of my best memories. He spoke to the hearts of the audience and, deeply moved by their enthusiastic Mediterranean response, extended his set. We took the time to share and celebrate.

George Benson was nine when he recorded his first record. After being an ambassador for rhythm and blues, he became the American idol of jazz funk. He plays the guitar like a god. His performance at the *Festival Jazz à l'Hospitalet* was amazing. I went to greet him in his dressing room after the concert. He asked for a glass of Chardonnay, and I suggested our Aigle Royal. We drank

---

*Claude Spanghero is a former French rugby union footballer. He was a part of the French side which won the Five Nations in 1973.

three bottles with his musicians while discussing his passion for French white wines. After a few glasses, he sang some of his best-known hits for us, and we enjoyed this timeless moment together. At his request, I sent a few cases of wine to his home in Arizona. I hope he'll be able to play at l'Hospitalet again during his next European tour.

Cali, my Catalan friend, has extraordinary sensitivity. He is a pure gem who transcends himself on stage, taking the audience with him as soon as he starts playing. I love his personality, generosity, and his incomparable style. I tasked him with organising original performances, inviting his artist friends for a unique show. That evening turned into a special moment because Cali can create an incredible alchemy with the audience, helped by the Big Band Brass, masterfully led by Dominique Rieux. Cali loves to party. Maybe because of his past life as a rugby player, he has a thrilling connection with the audience during his performances, and afterward with the happy few who are not ready to go to bed yet. These precious, shared moments fill our hearts. Cali has become the embodiment of the mindset of this festival, which owes its success to the kind and honest proximity between the artists and the audience. We enjoy putting the world to rights and playing, late at night, the best tunes of his idol, Bono, the singer of U2, the legendary band.

We always keep a few surprises for our friends. The world of rugby is celebrated at Château l'Hospitalet. Lately, we've had the privilege to organise a masterclass on the theme of excellence with legends of the last World Cups: Richie McCaw, captain of a twice-world-champion team; Tendai Mtawarira, a Springbok nicknamed the Beast of South Africa; and our national star, Thierry Dusautoir. This magical evening celebrated fraternity, solidarity, and the values of rugby. These men have high expectations of themselves and embody individual performance in the service of a collective cause. Their affectionate and emotional personalities give them an aura, a radiance serving an ideal much bigger than themselves. We need them to bear witness to their ability to live together and cultivate their differences to better serve the team, so that we can turn it into an example of integration and respect for different cultures.

The world of wine is also a place of inspiring encounters. Jancis Robinson has become the most influential woman in wine. She has tirelessly travelled the world, using her expert knowledge and the rigour born out of her qualification as a Master of Wine. Jancis has contributed to the sharing of wine culture worldwide with unparalleled expertise, deep humanity, and an encyclopaedic knowledge of wine. Our tastings over the last three decades have always been rich, shared moments. At the end of a long tasting of red wines, I gave her a toothbrush and homeopathic toothpaste to help her get rid of the stains left on her teeth by tannin deposits. She laughed at this unexpected gift. She wrote about the incident on her site, and an Australian dentist commented that toothpaste after a tasting is bad for tooth enamel. With her typical British sense of humour, she wondered if she should sue me. This joke makes us laugh whenever we meet. She loves our part of the world, where she often stays to recuperate and write books such as *The World Atlas of Wine*. She is also a big jazz fan, another connection.

Kyriakos Kynigopoulos, originally from Greece but now a

world citizen and a respected ambassador for Burgundy wines, has become one of the greatest oenologists alive. I met him on a beach in Thessaloniki, and we developed a professional and friendly relationship. With his faithful sidekick, Pierre Fonteneau, he helps us make wine at the Domaine de l'Aigle. We have learned to get the best from Chardonnay and Pinot Noir through changing harvest dates, vinification, and maturation. He is brilliant at getting teams to work together. Guillaume Barraud, Thibaut Haentjens, and their teams now use Burgundian methods to achieve excellence with the wines of the estate. A few details make a big difference for the enjoyment of those who drink our wines.

Michel Rolland was the first flying winemaker. He developed his expertise worldwide and gained international renown in the art and skills needed to make great wines. I always enjoy the rare moments we share together, as well as his wine culture, which he puts at the service of the best winegrowers wherever they may be. These are always delicious moments spent with him at the best restaurants with exceptional wines. He is gifted at bringing together personalities such as Alain Dominique Perrin, winegrower at Château Lagrézette in Cahors, founder of the Fondation Cartier; Andreas Larsson, best sommelier in the world; and Jean Luc Roché and Pascal Payraudeau, founders of wine fairs in French supermarkets.

Marvin Shanken, the founder of the American magazine *Wine Spectator*, managed to create a media empire in wine and spirits and later in the art of cigar smoking. I first met him at lunch in his dining room in New York, with his editor Thomas Matthew, when he told me about his struggles to create a wine culture in the USA. His passion for collecting, his love for France, and especially of the painter Toulouse-Lautrec, brought us together when I bought the Château de Céleyran, in the La Clape mountains where Toulouse-Lautrec spent part of his youth and celebrated the culture of the Languedoc and its origins in Roman civilisation in his paintings.

The Roman origins of Narbonne - Narbo Martius, founded in 111 BC - are now told by Jacques Michaud, a tireless ambassador of our region and brilliant speaker. We have developed a brother-like friendship and founded together the *Confrérie des Chevaliers de l'Art de Vivre*, which, every year, inducts the most faithful ambassadors of our region and its wines. It is very important to celebrate and share the love of our land with celebrities in the world of wine, art, economy, sports, and show business.

I've always loved meeting great chefs in Paris. I have a special affection for the living legends, Guy Savoy and Alain Ducasse. I love dining in Guy Savoy's kitchen and sharing with him precious gastronomical and friendly moments. Guy is a tireless advocate of French terroirs and products. We share the values of rugby and the impertinence of those who've had to earn their stripes on the field, fuelled by an appetite for conquest and the will to surprise diners. Guy has the panache and fieriness of those who know that excellence resides in the smallest details. Alain Ducasse is an emperor who matches tastes and trends with virtuosity and imagination. A tireless culinary innovator, he brings together, with great precision, food and wine in a setting where magic sublimates the experience. His boundless curiosity transports people into his universe, and his inspiration is always ahead of its time.

Claude Onesta, the most awarded French sports coach, several times European, World, and Olympic handball champion, has joined the circle of friends of l'Hospitalet. I admire his vision of managing people and the art of enhancing team spirit to serve a cause that goes beyond the individual egos of each athlete. I have learned a lot from our discussions, his sense of camaraderie, and his high standards when it comes to performance. With Pierre Dantin, his friend and partner, they succeeded in earning the trust of the French Olympic teams during a moment of national unity celebrating the victories of our champions.

The road to success

Life is an experience that, after failures, can bring pleasant surprises and great joys. The education given to me by my father, Georges, and my mother, Geneviève, the family ambiance around my grandmother, Paule – the cornerstone of the family – and the passions I followed with wine and rugby have shaped my personality and given structure to my life. I drew a lot of strength from the unconditional family love I received, the care of my mother, and the drive of my father towards a better future. Rugby was my raison d'être for twenty-five years.

I did my military service at the *École Interarmées des Sports* in Fontainebleau after finishing my studies in Toulouse. As captain of the French Army team, I continued my training, practising sport four to five hours a day. Despite my constant back-and-forth between Fontainebleau and Narbonne and missing the club's training sessions, I found my place in the team. I had to earn the trust of the older players and the respect of our adversaries. Narbonne was a well-known and respected team. We were young but determined. We were hungry for success. We won the Yves du Manoir challenge three times and took part in the finals eight years running. Some of us were selected to play for France.

I played my last season at the Stade Français in Paris, where I was captain. Joining this new adventure rejuvenated me. The president, an unconventional visionary, changed the mentality of rugby and turned it into a spectator's sport. Thanks to him, French rugby entered a new era.

At the age of thirty, and after ten seasons at the highest level, it was time for me to put an end to my career, as my body was beginning to show signs of fatigue. During all these years, I have managed my sport career and the development of my professional activities. The year spent in Paris was key as it enabled me to meet Max Guazzini, a show business supremo in charge of the programme of the NRJ Group, the main radio in the country. His genius for communication and keen marketing acumen opened my eyes to the needs of consumers. During these exciting years, I had the opportunity to develop professional and friendly relationships with many decision-makers in the world of wine distribution. Sport, and especially rugby, are great door openers.

I meant to spend more time with my family and my wife, whom I had just married. Fate had other plans though. While at the 1995 World Cup final in Johannesburg between the Springboks, then the world champions, and the All Blacks, I went to a night club with my friends Pierre Rougon and Jean-Pierre Andlauer to discuss the game. François Sangalli, a former player from Narbonne, joined us at one o'clock in the morning, and we started talking about the Narbonne club. For two hours, I shared my vision with him as well as the changes I thought would improve the club's performance. As I was leaving at three o'clock, Jean-Louis Barsalou, the new president of the club, arrived. After telling him about our discussion and my ideas, François added, "You should take Gérard with you to manage the club." This rather bizarre set of circumstances decided my new mission with my beloved club. Destiny had intervened. I spent the following three years dividing my time between my job as a winegrower, my new company, and my all-consuming passion to propel the Narbonne club into professional rugby. I learned a lot from this time. From a sporting point of view, we had good results, being one of the best five French clubs.

To preside over a professional rugby club at the age of thirty is an opportunity but also a burden. I was full of new ideas and motivated by boundless enthusiasm. Despite the club's good results, I was met with power struggles I was ill-equipped to solve and which ended up being detrimental to the good running of the club. These difficult times toughened me up and made me gain ten years in maturity. The experience allowed me to enter the real world of business and lose a form of naivety. I learnt from it and moved on after three years to dedicate myself to my wine activities.

My ambition was clear, but I kept it a secret as I didn't have the critical size yet to share my plan: creating an innovative and international brand, based on the culture of the area and able to compete with the greatest wines in the world.

My small team of fifteen people was tight and full of determination. I couldn't reveal my goals yet as they would have seemed far too ambitious. For wine, as for rugby, I didn't set myself any limits as I had a clear vision of the potential of my terroir. Methodically, I visited all French distributors, offering them new ideas. At the weekends, we organised in-store promotions and I didn't take any holidays for ten years. Our high level of debt meant we had to be constantly on the move and generating growth. The successive takeovers of various estates and the development of the Gérard Bertrand brand strengthened our commercial offer. My friend Peter Darbyshire, vice-president of the group for twelve years, helped me to create a clear marketing strategy and to create value. Evolving from a production-based company to a sales and marketing company was a decisive step. The purchase of Château l'Hospitalet gave credibility to our progress. Our banking partners supported us as they trusted us and had faith in our company.

Success is always in proportion to the risks undertaken. It stimulates energy and helps you to feel alive. I always trusted in my lucky star and invested all my efforts in this conquest of the world. I gave the company the financial and commercial means to launch myself in this competition. I had confidence in the quality of our wines, but I also vouched for our capacity to innovate. We had to develop our distribution network and place our region on the map of the wines of the world.

Success is always in proportion to the risks undertaken. It stimulates energy and helps you to feel alive. I always trusted in my lucky star and invested all my efforts in this conquest of the world.

Georges Frêche, president of the Languedoc-Roussillon region, after consultation, launched the idea of promoting Sud de France, an umbrella brand linking together AOPs, IGPs*, and all quality designation. With large financial resources, this federation of

---

*AOP : Appellation d'Origine Contrôlée.
IGP : Indication Géographique Protégée.

generic bodies started spending budgets worthy of other great wine areas. The positioning of Sud de France, its positive image, and its obvious localisation were considerable assets in creating consumer demand. Some didn't see it that way and put the brakes on this brilliant idea. We didn't hesitate and continued to promote the region and its lifestyle. We went even further and created the segmentation of organic wines by launching sulphite-free, bee-friendly, and biodynamic wines. We also contributed to the launch of wines in the process of conversion to organic farming to convince new winegrowers to join us. We signed a partnership with the winegrowers of the Vergèze cooperative cellar and their fantastic president, Jean-Frédéric Coste. Investing over fifteen million euros to create the most beautiful cellar in Europe dedicated to our region and based on organic farming was betting on the future, a daring bet that we supported and helped manage.

The 2000s were fertile ground for development. The economic situation in France and the world was good, and consumers were getting more curious to discover new production areas. The Languedoc evolved slowly from a value position to a more premium one, offering greater pleasure and sophistication to wine consumers. The *Gault & Millau* panel of judges, wine fairs promoted by *La Revue des Vins de France*, or the magazine *Le Point* were a great springboard for our wines in France. In Europe, varietal wines were very much in demand. The recognition of our Crus by the INAO* allowed us to create a terroir and value hierarchy. New

*Institut national de l'origine et de la qualité, INAO is responsible for the implementation of French policy on official signs of identification of the origin and quality of agricultural and food products.

markets opened, from ten to fifty within less than ten years. At great speed, we invested in our teams, structures, and ultra-modern equipment to ensure the constant renewal of quality, the improvement of traceability, and know-how. This dynamic, through creating new opportunities, made the Gérard Bertrand brand and its wines stronger and allowed us to expand worldwide. We knew how to listen to our partners and distributors and help them to implement large promotional mechanisms.

The 2008 financial crisis put the brakes on export to the USA. Our importer collapsed into administration. Far from being disheartened, I embarked on a tour of the country with Peter Darbyshire to find another partner. The reactions were sometimes stinging: “It’s not the right time, you have too many lines” or worse, “Wines from the South of France are not high-quality enough.” Doors closed in our faces. On our way back, I told my vice-president that we’d start our own importing company. This daring bet changed the story of our group. Our failure to convince American importers turned out to be a blessing in disguise as it allowed us to discuss freely with distributors and supermarket chains. We started with just two people. For ten years, I travelled in person, to each state, visiting the main distributors to convince them. Our range of estate wines met with a lot of success. The big change finally arrived with our range of rosé wines that gained a foothold everywhere in the country and soon found itself in all sales outlets. The role of Mel Dick, Senior Vice-president with Southern Wine & Spirits, was key. This visionary man felt my passion and my determination to conquer the American market. He took me under his wing, guided me, and introduced me to the largest decision-makers in the USA. One of them was Annette Alvarez Peters, the most influential woman over there, in charge of buying for Costco, the number one retailer in North America. She was the first to launch our rosé in all her stores.

Being open to the magic of encounters, being a good listener, and having a bit of cheek to attract curiosity and kindness, is how we shape our destiny. Succeeding in the USA created a halo effect that radiated not just in America but globally. We built up our local teams and now have over twenty people working there. Canada also became a priority market receptive to our new initiatives. The snowball effect ensured our growth and ongoing dynamism for the next fifteen years.

In 2019, I was invited to join the president of the French Republic on his official trip to China. We participated in the official visits, notably the inauguration of the Shanghai exhibition. To my great surprise, a food and wine tasting was planned for the two presidents. They sampled four different types of French beef - Aubrac, Limousine, Charolaise, and Salers - paired with red wines from grands crus from Bordeaux, Burgundy, and Château l'Hospitalet. At the end of the tasting, president Xi Jinping told president Macron that the fourth wine, mine, was his favourite. The French president invited me to join the conversation and gave a thorough presentation of my wine, noting it was from the South of France and made from biodynamic grapes grown next to the Mediterranean Sea. Xi Jinping asked me for the price of the wine; he looked very pleased. International media, television, and radio recorded this interaction, transforming our sales in China. We increased our distribution and recruited eight people to promote our wines in this vast country.

Over the last fifteen years, our group has grown from eighty to four hundred and fifty people. My highly valued managing director, Michael Van Duijn, oversees the back office while I remain in charge of the front office, wine quality, and business development. We created different departments to meet the demands of our markets and support the internationalisation of the group. We have recruited talented experts in hospitality and data management to improve the client experience We have developed a culture of operational excellence, implemented processes that guarantee smooth business operations, and created a 'brand factory,' an experimental laboratory responsible for research and development and the creation of new products to meet the needs of new consumers and diverse drinking occasions. This is similar to what spirits groups that specialise in new consumption trends do. The development of *apéritifs* in Europe and happy hours in America has shaken up the drinking habits of both young and older consumers. Cocktails now compete with sparkling and chilled wines. The success of these offers has led to a decline in wine sales, especially at the bar counter. We launched a range of lower alcohol wine-based cocktails to meet this new demand, creating a bold new category. One evening in a bar in Tokyo with Jan Visser, my Asia Pacific sales director, and Clément Carrière-Pradal, my international sales director, we ordered a glass of sake before dinner. The waiter brought us a cloudy drink. The unexpected colour, cloudiness, and taste of the drink caught my attention. I had a revelation and told my teammates, "This is the concept we need to emulate: let's launch a range of unfiltered wines where taste and freshness will carry and strengthen aromatic expression. This way, we create a new tasting experience with a specific and slightly rough texture, a different feeling".

This challenge turned out to be a real headache for my teams, but they eventually succeeded and created the Trouble XP brand, a quirky drink that meets the expectations of the new generation of drinkers. It opened the door to a new world of expressions, complementing the classicism of the great terroir wines, and contributing to the growing outreach of our group.

It had become important to communicate our lifestyle, values, and the specificities of our terroir to consumers and wine lovers, who are often thirsty for product knowledge. Founding the five-star Wine Resort Beach & Spa at Château l'Hospitalet supports our premiumisation strategy. We offer a unique experience to the clients with the masterclass room, boutique, and themed restaurants. Chez Paule is dedicated to the traditional recipes of my grandmother, while Hospitalet Beach promotes Mediterranean cuisine during the summer months. L'Art de Vivre, recently awarded an Étoile Verte Michelin award, serves 'vertical cuisine'. This innovative concept, created by Chef Laurent Chabert and our sommelier, Pierre-Alexis Mengual, aims to find the perfect

'Vertical cuisine' reveals the true taste of terroir and stimulates the senses while creating a unique vibration and reinvented freshness, offering classical or rule-breaking food and wine pairings.

balance between seasonality, ingredients, and terroirs. Produce is sourced from the Celeyran biodynamic farm and cooked without cream or butter to create an airy sensation. 'Vertical cuisine' reveals the true taste of terroir and stimulates the senses while creating a unique vibration and reinvented freshness, offering rule-breaking food and wine pairings. This concept, unique in the world, is taken even further and magnified in the Moon Room, where it puts into perspective the terrestrial and cosmic multidimensionality of human beings. Experiencing 'vertical cuisine' reveals our links to the universe and harmonises our 'chakras' through drinking biodynamic wines, influenced by the moon, the sun, planets, and musical frequencies. The sublimated lifestyle offered in this mindfulness oasis is an invitation to let go, experience emotional sublimation, and foster a communion of minds among guests.

We also developed a new method to produce orange wines (skin contact white wines) while adhering to the age-old philosophy and know-how of winemakers from Georgia in Eastearn Europe, and utilising vinification and maturation techniques that transformed the quality of these wines. By reducing their bitterness and tannin levels, we enhanced their balance, structure, and aromatic expression. Orange Gold, Genora, and Villa Soleilla are a new generation of orange wines that perfectly match cooked vegetables, strongly flavoured fish, or, more traditionally, cheese.

For thirty years, day after day, year after year, I have maintained my appetite for conquest and discovery of new markets for our wines. Transforming from a winegrower to the managing director of a large company was only possible thanks to a faithful and talented team, boundless imagination, and an unusual strength of conviction. This determination was fuelled by sport, especially rugby, blending the virtues of a fighting character with a family spirit. A company can also be like a tribe or a clan that shares the same goal and ideal. I have always enjoyed enthusing people, creating a new paradigm based on the values of solidarity and fraternity. The strength of love and human qualities, founded on the virtues of compassion and sharing, create a heartfelt yearning that fosters a sense of belonging typical of the wine trade.

A commercial strategy is prepared much like a military campaign. Everything starts with identifying the mission's goal, priority objectives, and products to market. When you come from a region without much recognition, you'd better be well prepared. "Aim far, strike fast" is our motto. We must remain true to our vision, build a clear strategy, and implement efficient action plans with sufficient means and ambitious goals. These are the five pillars of success. They are not taught in business schools but learned in the school of life.

The most beautiful conquest is to break free from one's past and upbringing and become a better version of oneself. To reach that level of consciousness and confidence, you need to push your limits and accept the challenge of putting yourself in danger. Getting out of one's comfort zone is where the adventure begins, and it is how one learns to have a broader vision, master stress, and develop the ability to persuade others. This inner strength grows with each difficulty that is overcome. Audacity and courage are two sides of the same coin. They complement each other and open up a field of possibilities. Obstacles on the path are opportunities for progress. One never loses; one learns. Successes should be analysed so they can be replicated and expanded. Methodology, organisation, and planning are essential to the successful implementation of any plan. Like in sport, you play the way you train. This approach is key in the business world too. An intervention should be carefully prepared, with holistic thinking and prioritised objectives.

At the beginning of a meeting, especially with a new prospect, asking three or four open-ended questions allows for a better understanding of the person in front of you. It is better to be flexible and ready to change the flow of the presentation if the answers do not fit the initial strategy. You never get a second chance to make a good first impression. A bright look in your eye, a firm handshake, an easy smile, clear expression, and the right tone guarantee a good start.

It's much easier to learn how to manage stress when you already have some experience and have pushed your limits, whether in your daily life or on the rugby pitch. Trust is only gained slowly but can be lost in an instant. It is a flame that needs to be nurtured, always based on sincerity, as only trusting relationships last.

Psychology is also an important tool, an X factor to use wisely. You quickly realise if the person you're talking to is open-minded and if there is a chance to develop a deep professional relationship, and possibly even a friendship. Sometimes you need to navigate a hostile environment when you do not share the same values or priorities. In such cases, you need to defuse negativity and create the right conditions for a loyal and constructive connection. Nothing is easy; everything must be deserved and earned.

The development of a brand entails different stages. The first is that of pioneers, those who do not realise their mission is impossible. You must keep the faith, maintain a hint of madness, and possess a strength of conviction that sweeps everything in its way. That's the spirit that Stéphane Durand, my comrade in arms, my accomplice, and my party buddy brought to our company. After working in insurance, he joined us and tackled the French hospitality market with optimism and hard work. He is one of those who propelled the group forward and successfully activated conquest plans. Eric Lacombe, his counterpart in the world of mass market retail, brought his professional knowledge and strong willpower to the team. Both have become great managers and have built solid and driven teams. Céline Deboskre and Amanda Robert complete the line-up.

Discipline and respect for basic rules complement the thirst for conquest. They create a unique space for freedom that allows you to achieve your desires and motivate other team members. I impose this routine on myself first: remain positive, eat healthily, and alternate between festive and frugal periods. Being a true Epicurean means practising this form of asceticism that allows you to enjoy life's pleasures while staying focused on your priorities.

When I decided to send Alistair Pine, a valiant Scotsman, to the USA, he embodied the values of generosity and faithfulness that reign supreme overseas. Starting from scratch was an exciting task. Bit by bit, we built a temple, a solid architecture, an achievement granted to those who never give up, regardless of the circumstances. Creating a new path and signposting it is a rare opportunity in one's life. I enjoy doing it whenever I can with an expanded team of experienced Americans and talented, enthusiastic French people like Mélanie Bacou, who went from strength to strength in the USA.

Success often rests on a utopia, a shared vision, an intuition that can change the established order.

Success often rests on a utopia, a shared vision, an intuition that can change the established order. There are perceptible tipping points that create new trends. One should never lose sight of the link between enthusiasm, altruism, and that peculiar feeling that makes an idea spread and reach category managers, the decision-makers responsible for discovering what doesn't yet exist. It is the spark that will ignite the fire and create a new demand from consumers.

In a more theoretical way, I have identified four steps to success: critical success, commercial success, brand power, and value creation. Each step is a specific moment in the story of entrepreneurs, their long-term vision, the relevance of their actions, and the power of their business model.

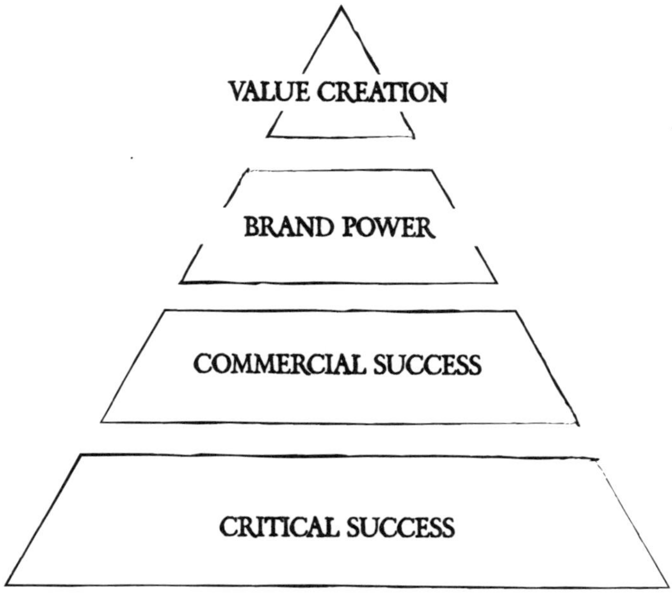

* THE PYRAMID OF SUCCESS *

The pyramid of success rests on the cornerstone of product quality supported by an authentic backstory.

I am grateful for the persistence, conviction, and sleepless nights of all those who have managed and sustained a vineyard or a business—often a family one—while taking good care of their staff and taking pride in their products or services, often without making much money. When the time comes to pass the baton to the next generation or to sell to a third party, these leaders can retire with a sense of accomplishment and the joy of having upheld a regional or national tradition. A good leader wins hearts and minds, earns the respect of customers, and secures the loyalty of suppliers. At the time of departure, this critical success ensures a smooth handover.

Commercial success requires the combination of several factors: ambition, competitive spirit, an appetite for growth, but also strength of character, commercial flair and the ability to seize market opportunities to work hand in hand with commercial partners and distributors. Beware however of the risk to let clients' priorities dictate the group's strategy, a classical pitfall especially for family companies.

In the world of wine, this approach is typical of companies that prioritise volume over value creation and, trapped by existing industrial investments, need to produce at full capacity to lower costs. Economic cycles are long. This modus operandi fits into the growth-oriented logic of the generation that developed these activities but is difficult to escape for the next generation. The more a company focuses on clients' needs without considering the end consumer, the less capacity it has to change its existing business model. It works as long as production costs remain low. In the case of a poor harvest or a steep increase in the cost of materials, margins tighten, and problems ensue. Leaders following this approach are true heroes of their country as they take risks, sustain industries, and meet the government's needs for low inflation.

A successful sector should include companies of all sizes and shapes

I chose not to follow that path because I envisioned a long-term strategy founded on value-based brands and meeting the needs of diverse consumer categories. In our case, the umbrella brand is the creator's name because it reflects a family story that began with my grandmother, Paule. The wine from her century-old Carignan parcel, named 'Les Arbousiers', was first marketed with the 2019 vintage and contributes to strengthening the original family values established on hard work, humility, and hope.

My father, Georges, was driven by a deep love for his land and a clear vision of its potential for development, but he was definitely ahead of his time. He never gave up and, with limited financial means, became a regional reference known for his courage, charisma, and tasting abilities. He was one of the first to implement parcel selection, trying to convince other winegrowers and teach them how to improve the quality of their wines. Transitioning from a hunting and gathering economy to a production economy was an important step towards a better future. However, Southern France lagged behind other regions already following the rules of the market economy. My father recognised this and often wrote to other stakeholders, emphasising that marketing should be a priority in the region's strategy. He saw it as a new way to promote regional wines while expressing the potential of each individual appellation. I was shaped by his work as a terroir discoverer and revealer of typicity and taste. My vision for our part of the world was refined by my travels, first in France - in Bordeaux, Champagne, and Burgundy - but even more so in the New World, in the USA, Argentina, Chile, and Australia.

In the 1990s, there were two contrasting visions of wine. In the Old World, everything was based on terroir and a classical hierarchical structure of prestigious estates and a few respected family companies such as the Rothschilds in France, Antinori and Frescobaldi in Italy, and Torres in Spain. In the New World, the innovative ideas of Robert Mondavi inspired me greatly. I was fortunate enough to meet him when I was twenty-three. He put California on the world wine map, promoted Cabernet Sauvignon as the king of grape varieties, developed oenotourism and wine routes, and created a collective spirit in his region to spread the American dream even further.

After ten years of learning the ropes in my wine career, it was time for me not just to be the heir of the Villemajou estate but to forge my own path. My father had dedicated his life to developing a collective of winegrowers and cooperative cellars. He fought hard to convince others and sometimes failed, so I chose a more personal path.

We are craftsmen and activists who champion a cause greater than ourselves. My time had come. In 1995, I started a new life and took the first step towards this existential quest dedicated to my region through branding. At the beginning of the adventure, we used intuition and common sense to create the first concepts—first to celebrate the different appellations, then to launch organic wines, and finally to develop the rosé category. Our strength of conviction and interpersonal skills earned the trust of the main French distributors. We developed the premium varietal wines category, first with Monoprix, then Carrefour and Auchan. Listing fifteen to twenty new wines with each enabled us to grow the company. By segmenting and creating a hierarchy for our offer, we developed the success of our premium wines. We were among the first to develop partnerships with mass retailers at a time when established French brands refused to work with them. I was always proud to create popular wines as they meet the needs of faithful yet demanding customers. It is much more difficult to maintain taste and quality consistency when you produce several million bottles sold on all five continents.

Languedoc wines gradually appeared on the wine lists of good restaurants. Gérard Margeon, head sommelier of the Alain Ducasse group, was the first to give me a chance and promote our estate wines in all the group's restaurants worldwide. Jean-Pierre Andlauer, Monoprix's buyer, also opened the way for me. Working with Antoine Peleyras from Carrefour enabled another significant leap forward for the group. The era around the millennium was ripe for innovations. Decision-makers could make quick decisions without the validation of expert panels or consultants. We were creative and reactive. A new concept could be ready in a few weeks.

It took fifteen years to achieve enduring success for our brands in Europe. 2008 marked the beginning of the American adventure. We had to think differently, strengthen our teams, and develop new, more international brands. After the successful launches of Autrement and Gris Blanc brands, we undertook an in-depth reflection. The packaging of Coté des Roses was a trigger as it embodied all the values of our region in an unexpected style of bottle and closure. The secret of success sometimes lies in simplicity. Aligning the name of a wine with the design of the bottle, naming it after a nearby beach, and adding a new glass closure that matched the bottle colour turned out to be ingredients for success. The whole world hailed this wine, and sales grew rapidly. The group entered a new dimension, and within ten years, we became the leading French brand in the USA. The support of distributors and commercial partners made all the difference. During this period, we grew from one hundred to three hundred employees and developed and structured the company.

Paul Correia, our expert, constantly improves our processes to guarantee the highest quality for all our wines, working closely with Stéphane Queralt. Both share my high standards and know that each bottle that leaves our cellars must please the consumer. Our motto is to always overdeliver. Olivier Roux, in charge of production, manages all our flows brilliantly. He ensures the smooth running of operations.

It was time to embed our premiumisation strategy without compromising the success of our bestsellers, the ranges that created our international success in 175 countries and with all types of customers, be they supermarkets, independent wine shops, restaurants, luxury hotels, airlines, cruise ships, duty-free shops, or online retailers. Today, we are proud to be the flagbearer for the region worldwide.

We began by investigating, conducting consumer surveys, and analysing demand segmentation while developing our offerings for emerging sectors, particularly luxury products and rare wines. Together with Karine Hamelin, our marketing director, we created bestsellers and explored new areas for two decades. We then identified consumer types worldwide, linking them to wines in our portfolio. This preliminary work helped our teams and distributors to build their 360-degree plans for the future.

Explorers seek pleasure wines that promote sharing and conviviality. They love our brands, especially our rosés. Activists are concerned about the planet, prefer drinking organic wines, and buy from committed winegrowers. Our organic wines - Change, Autrement, Naturae, Solar 6, and Prima Nature - meet their need for mindful consumption. Traditionalists enjoy discovering history, terroir, region, and generational and cultural heritage. Our Heritage range, designed to showcase all the appellations from Southern France, caters to this need. Connoisseurs look for characterful wines with typicity, strong taste identity, and an emotional response to the spirit of a place. This mindset aligns with our estate wines collection, which captures the essence of each individual estate. Collectors, an expert minority, respond to the message carried by a bottle of wine within the framework of a rare and subtle experience. Our iconic wines - Clos d'Ora, Clos du Temple, Villa Soleilla - as well as our Legend Vintage collection of *vins doux naturels*, meet this quest for excellence.

This meticulous work of matching market needs with our product range structure does not negate our heritage or expertise. It gives meaning and direction to our strategy and that of our partners. After struggling for twenty years to sell an idea, a dream, and a destination - Southern France - we moved to the next stage of hierarchisation and defining drinking occasions. This brand architecture clearly and comprehensively represents the diversity of our offer and lays the foundations to communicate with consumers.

This meticulous work of matching market needs with our product range structure does not negate our heritage or expertise. It gives meaning and direction to our strategy and that of our partners.

The role of Véronique Braun, our communications director, is crucial in devising detailed plans, especially in our ten main markets, and splitting our investment between importers and retailers. We also continually improve our hospitality and share our expertise. Promoting the French spirit and securing a prime position in this globalised universe requires a lot of thought, clarity, and precise timing. France is a country of tradition and elegance, with an extraordinary historical and cultural heritage, a unique lifestyle, and world-class companies such as LVMH, Kering, Chanel, and Hermès. These groups contribute to the image and influence of our civilisation. The great wines from Bordeaux, Burgundy, Champagne, and the great spirits brands from Cognac structure the wine and spirits industry and make France an indispensable tourism destination. The attractiveness of our country is remarkable; we are the most visited country in the world.

Occitania is rich in the diversity of its landscapes, architectural treasures, gastronomy, and wines. Because wine drinkers are becoming increasingly demanding and enjoy exploring a variety of wines, our strategy is based on offering several levels of product ranges to suit every drinking occasion.

The strength of the Gérard Bertrand company lies in its visceral and emotional attachment with each category. We are not always talking to the same people, but the idea is to maintain an intergenerational and cultural connection with all of them. I am inspired by the segmentation devised by Armani, a self-made man in the world of fashion: it rests on a strong origin, unique know-how, boundless creativity, successful diversification, and timelessness that ensures longevity.

Experiencing our hospitality, whether at our own places, in flight, on cruise ships, in premium hotels, or top restaurants, has created a desirability that enhances the pleasure of drinking our wines at home. The artistic direction and social media ecosystems developed by my daughter, Emma Bertrand, and her team meet this desire for proximity with wine lovers, who enjoy sharing experiences from all over the world in real time.

"Think global and act local" is a universal motto that perfectly addresses the needs of the wine industry and offers a path to success. We are on our way, and it is genuinely exciting. We still have many wines to invent, consumers to surprise, experts to convert, and prospects to convince. "If you want to plough a straight furrow, hitch your plough to a star," wrote the author Guy de Larigaudie. That is our credo.

The framework of our strategy is set, and I am its guarantor.

Implementing our plan involves deploying our commercial teams - over seventy people strong - across five continents, efficiently supporting our distributors' teams and creating an emotional bond with wine drinkers.

Once this preparatory work is done, each of our employees will need to find the necessary energy and enthusiasm to meet their own goals, whether in the vineyard or when working with consumers. The power of brands and their bond with consumers determine the financial health of companies and their valuation, especially for publicly traded companies. For family companies, particularly in the wine industry, land and asset value is an indicator dependent on the attractiveness of a region, its future potential, the prestige of its appellations, and the image of its estates. Bordeaux and Champagne were the first to register openly valued transactions in the last thirty years. In the past ten years, Burgundy has slowly transitioned from a farming business model to a speculative business model. Northern Rhône, Châteauneuf-du-Pape, and Provence have followed suit. The Loire and Languedoc are still undervalued, but icons are emerging. The recent sale of Clos Rougeard in the Loire, the rise in value of the Pic-Saint-Loup, and Terrasses du Larzac appellations in Languedoc are opening new paths. Our investments over the past twenty years, our international distribution, and the worldwide reputation of Clos du Temple, Clos d'Ora, Villa Soleilla, and Château l'Hospitalet mean we are now allocating our top wines among our distributors to reach the most discerning wine drinkers on earth.

Having some of our wines voted Best in the World several times by influential magazines and competitions such as *Decanter, the International Wine Challenge, Drinks Business*, and *Le Figaro* enhances the status of our group and our estates, the reputation of our know-how and sustainable viticultural methods, and the global reputation of the South of France.

Time is the best ally of winegrowers; the history of estates is often transgenerational.

Time is the best ally of winegrowers; the history of estates is often transgenerational. The best outcome for a winegrower is transmission, as long as it is anticipated and thought out, and that the new generation is trained in a spirit of continuity with a dash of innovation. There are no set rules; all the main French and international wine regions face the same dilemma. Developing iconic wines with solid distribution helps to secure a successful transmission. It is the final stage of the pyramid of success.

The ultimate experience

Every individual has their own personal challenge to face. Sometimes, we encounter multiple challenges, adding excitement to life. We all have the potential to be multidimensional, yet we are also human and therefore limited. Our impulses, feelings, and emotions guide our lives. Education, lifestyle, family, and school environments are key factors in shaping our identity, but each person is unique and must understand their own purpose in life. The best way to achieve one's dreams is to take action. Theory and self-knowledge are valuable assets that stem from a classical education. Those who succeed dream big and visualise their lives.

Undoubtedly, there will be obstacles and poor advice along the way. It is often wiser to keep one's dreams private, especially when they may seem mad or unrealistic to others. No one else can live my life. I have had to learn the difference between passing moods and deep convictions. To do so, I developed the ability to listen and understand myself. 'Man, know thyself and you will know the Universe and the Gods,' reads the inscription on the temple of Delphi, illustrating the long and winding path to finding one's special destiny. The fiery innocence of youth enabled me to take the first steps towards my destiny with the strength needed to take off. Early successes, even minor ones, gave me the confidence to go further. Faith multiplied my courage, even if it sometimes turned into a form of impertinence and impatience in my early years.

My sports career, the battles on the rugby field, individual and collective challenges, and the celebrations that followed shaped me and developed my strong personality. They gave me the certainty that 'Alone, I go faster; together, we go further.' Rugby is akin to life. Whatever your physique, character, or personality, when you connect with others and strive for the same goals, you are invincible. This heartfelt commitment, felt when putting oneself in danger, opens the door to a new awareness. Struggles are essential to growth, excellence, daily improvement, forging one's certainties, refining one's personality, and later, becoming more tolerant and patient. Rugby, this human adventure, powered the first thirty years of my life.

The time for change and great ambitions came in 1995. No longer did I have to juggle my two passions, wine and rugby, according to the seasons, or manage my priorities between the autumn harvest and spring blending. My new course was set. I secretly aspired to achieve what no one had managed in the Languedoc: to create a resilient company with the personal, financial, and technical means to withstand the vagaries of nature and difficult harvests, and then to develop international brands imbued with values and commitment, offering wine drinkers a fantastic experience. I aimed to create categories for South of France wines globally and to gain recognition for our terroirs and crus. The challenge was enormous, and I had a long way to go. I remain determined to make the most of my blending talent, my resolve, and my unwavering belief that this region is the most beautiful in the world, rich with treasures to share.

After painstakingly conquering the French market, we expanded into European markets with a clear, segmented offer: rosés becoming fashionable drinks, organic wines representing a complex, differentiated offer, especially in biodynamics, and our estate wines aspiring to be on the world's best restaurant lists. We climbed each mountain in turn, not without struggles but with support from far-sighted international customers like Jacques Wein-Depot in Germany, Sligro in the Netherlands, Air France and Norwegian Cruise Line in the USA. They understood the potential of our wines and were the first to share their terroir typicity with their customers.

The conquering years from 1990 to 2010 earned us legitimacy and market recognition, allowing us to weave an invisible global network carrying our values, our DNA, and the 'taste of somewhere.' Each victory contributed to our global conquest. By 2010, we were established, known, and respected in the wine world but not yet part of the international wine aristocracy. People were curious about us, respected us, but also feared or misunderstood us. I realised I had to earn my stripes through hard work, a challenge I was prepared for from my past as a high-level athlete.

Success and recognition, when they come, are not due to avoided struggles but to those tackled head-on. Each challenge leads to the ultimate goal. Part of our strategy was to choose the best distributors, not necessarily the biggest, but those with networks suited to different types of distribution. The global wine market is very segmented, complex, and has different expectations depending on countries, traditions, customs rules,

Success and recognition, when they come, are not due to avoided struggles but to those tackled head-on.

and purchasing power. We became experts in market strategy. After decades of travelling the world, I developed friendships and good relationships with many influential personalities, including key decision-makers in France, Europe, Canada, the USA, and the travel retail sector, now the sixth continent.

Listening to and understanding the commercial and logistical functioning and priorities of different markets, alongside competing with spirits and beer giants, is a genuine challenge. Everyone wants to understand the expectations of new wine drinkers, and gain a foothold in their chosen drinking moments, often outside mealtimes. Large spirits groups burst with creativity, unlike small, often traditional wine companies. The last significant wine success was the massive increase in rosé consumption, driven by Brad Pitt and Angelina Jolie in Provence. We rode that wave with our popular, fashionable wines.

Champagne, post-Covid, recovered through a new segmentation of its offer. Managing growth in this region, while cultivating the values of French heritage, is a source of inspiration. The dominant positions of the LVMH group and Pernod-Ricard ensure the enduring cultural influence of the French spirit worldwide. Our strategy in the early 2010s was clear: create world-class wines that could rival icons like Vega Sicilia, Sassicaia, Opus One, or Grange, combining exceptional terroirs, tested know-how, old vines, unique cellars, and selective distribution.

After successfully placing La Forge, Le Viala, L'Hospitalitas, and Aigle Royal on the best wine lists worldwide over fifteen years, the next stage was to join the legendary top wines from Bordeaux, Burgundy, and Northern Rhône.

The first of three steps was the launch of Clos d'Ora, a magical site on a geological fault at the top of the village of La Livinière. The four Mediterranean grape varieties—Syrah, Grenache, Mourvèdre, and Carignan—thrive here. The high altitude protects the grapes from overripening, adding freshness and longevity to the wine. The clay-limestone soils ensure typicity and adaptation of the grape varieties to the soil type. Biodynamic farming and animal presence, mules and ewes, reinforce its character and unique expression. The restoration by architect Jean-Frédéric Luscher of the old sheep barn demolished during the Second World War placed the estate among the best wine tourism destinations. After several vintages, the wine now ranks among the world's greats, contributing to the global recognition of Languedoc's finest red wines.

The Clos du Temple answers to another priority and a different timeframe. Elevating rosés into the category of great wines was a challenge that needed to be undertaken. Defining the taste of the terroir and the aging potential of the wine seemed like an impossibility, exactly the type of challenge I love to take on. With very old vines, an exceptional terroir, our proven know-how, an architectural temple like no other, and an irresistible desire to create a unique wine in a

Elevating rosés into the category of great wines was a challenge that needed to be undertaken. Defining the taste of the terroir and the aging potential of the wine seemed like an impossibility, exactly the type of challenge I love to take on.

singular setting with a bottle designed to transcend history, this wine sails beyond the boundaries of imagination and changes the conventions of colour, allowing the rosé category to gain legitimacy. When a wine is well-born, you know it, you feel it. The rest belongs to history and time. Its legend will grow, adding to its emotional charge and turn it into an icon, if all goes to plan.

The final step focuses on orange wines, made from a unique plot overlooking the Mediterranean Sea near Château l'Hospitalet. Villa Soleilla is the new iconic reference for orange wines. This amber-coloured drink, invented by the Georgians 8,000 years ago, bridges the freshness of white wines and the structure of reds. Vinifying white grapes like reds, leaving whole bunches to macerate, brings bitterness, structure, texture, and a long finish. This opens new communication avenues. Education is ongoing, supported by enthusiastic winegrowers and innovative food and wine pairings by chefs and sommeliers. Finding one perfect match with a platter of cheeses is an impossible task considering the differences between a goat's cheese, a camembert, a semi-hard or a blue cheese. Only orange wine works with all these strong characters. The same applies to spicy food, vegetables in sauce, lamb curry or great classical dishes such as osso buco or tagine. Villa Soleilla, made from Roussanne, Vermentino, and Viognier, derives strength and expression from its unique limestone terroir and twelve months in barrel. The challenge is motivating, and feedback from opinion makers confirms our decisions were right. Orange is the new black, with wine, like a sunset, sharing its original fragrance, textured deliciousness, and long-lasting pleasure.

Villa Soleilla and Château l'Hospitalet also symbolise the rise in prominence of our hotel and restaurant business. From the outset, I wanted to share our lifestyle concept. Turning our hotel into a five-star wine resort propelled us into a new dimension.

Château La Sauvageonne, overlooking a hill and surrounded by wild nature, is a serene space I find very moving. The villa on top is a calm place inviting celebration. In the south and the north, white and red grape varieties are planted together: Roussanne, Vermentino, Grenache Blanc and Viognier for the whites, Grenache Noir, Mourvèdre and Syrah for the reds. These vines are rooted in volcanic soils surrounded by schists. The landscape is like a natural symphony and the high altitude, and the steep slopes ensure a cool and sunny climate. The brute force of the elements and the power of the soils made us want to create two unique wines. We aimed to create a great Mediterranean white wine with ageing potential, and the first vintage exceeded expectations. The 2021 red is a harmonious blend of power, grace, elegance and expression of the biotope of the wine. Red and black fruit come first to the nose, followed by *garrigue*, mineral and spicy notes. The structure in the mouth is delicate, with a silky and lively texture and a very long finish. This wine has an impressive ageing potential. It contributes to the prestige of the Terrasses du Larzac.

These two wines have a unique history and required ten years of work before the first bottle could be released. The initial concept was filtered by the passage of time, small progress, moments of doubt but also exalting moments. One must always keep one's promises and stick to one's initial ambitious goals in this kind of project.

Iconic wines are the final step before legendary wines. The path between the two is narrow, and few will be chosen. The strength of honesty, ageing potential, and legendary meals make these wines sacred. Some fall from their pedestal and lose their shine. They only made a strong impression for a few years. Others remain at the top, shining for connoisseurs and collectors. These wines embody excellence in regions like France, Italy, Spain, Portugal, and the New World. Very occasionally, a few wines rise even higher, reaching a state of weightlessness and offering transcendental mindfulness. Romanée-Conti is one such wine, a meditation wine expressing a transcendental message. There are only a few winegrowers in the world who have developed the keen spiritual ability needed to reach the perfect vibration when all senses are in harmony.

Climbing the ladder of success has been my life's journey. It required asceticism, humility, ambition, connections, passion, and spirituality. This ladder sometimes feels like a mystical experience connecting me to the universe. I've learned to enjoy the euphoria of the peaks without arrogance, as the path was long and tough. My determination never wavered, and my goals remained unchanged. The most faithful team members are still with me, motivated and proud of our achievements.

I still have a few surprises in store, to be revealed when destiny decides.

CONTENTS

Gérard Bertrand SPH – Route de Narbonne Plage – 11100 Narbonne

ISBN : 978-2-9583515-7-1

First published in France under the title 'Le vin multidimensionnel' by Éditions Origine Nature.

British Library Cataloguing-in-Publication Data.
A catalogue record for this book is available from the British Library.

Editorial Management: Éditions Origine Nature.
Translation: Anne Burchett
Cover and Layout: Fourbi
Portrait of the cover page: ©David Fritz Goeppinger.

Printed in France by La Manufacture d'histoires DEUX-PONTS for Éditions Origine Nature, Narbonne, Occitanie, France.

MIX Paper FSC FSC® C128937

EDITIONS ORIGINE nature